I0199686

INDEX TO
CITY AND REGIONAL
MAGAZINES
OF THE
UNITED STATES

Recent Titles of
Historical Guides to the World's Periodicals and Newspapers

This series provides historically focused narrative and analytical profiles of periodicals and newspapers with accompanying bibliographical data.

British Literary Magazines: The Romantic Age, 1789-1836
Alvin Sullivan, editor

British Literary Magazines: The Victorian and Edwardian Age, 1837-1913
Alvin Sullivan, editor

Children's Periodicals of the United States
R. Gordon Kelly, editor

International Film, Radio, and Television Journals
Anthony Slide, editor

Science Fiction, Fantasy, and Weird Fiction Magazines
Marshall B. Tymn and Mike Ashley, editors

American Indian and Alaska Native Newspapers and Periodicals, 1925-1970
Daniel F. Littlefield, Jr., and James W. Parins, editors

Magazines of the American South
Sam G. Riley

Religious Periodicals of the United States: Academic and Scholarly Journals
Charles H. Lippy, editor

British Literary Magazines: The Modern Age, 1914-1984
Alvin Sullivan, editor

American Indian and Alaska Native Newspapers and Periodicals, 1971-1985
Daniel F. Littlefield, Jr., and James W. Parins, editors

Index to Southern Periodicals
Sam G. Riley

American Literary Magazines: The Eighteenth and Nineteenth Centuries
Edward E. Chielens, editor

American Humor Magazines and Comic Periodicals
David E. E. Sloane, editor

INDEX TO CITY AND REGIONAL MAGAZINES OF THE UNITED STATES

Compiled by

Sam G. Riley

and

Gary W. Selnow

Historical Guides to the World's Periodicals and Newspapers

Greenwood Press
New York • Westport, Connecticut • London

Library of Congress Cataloging-in-Publication Data

Riley, Sam G.
    Index to city and regional magazines of the United States /
compiled by Sam G. Riley and Gary W. Selnow.
        p. cm. — (Historical guides to the world's periodicals and
newspapers, ISSN 0742-5538)
        ISBN 0-313-26839-8 (lib. bdg. : alk. paper)
        1. American periodicals—Bibliography—Union lists.
        2. Journalism, Regional—United States—Bibliography—Union lists.
        3. Catalogs, Union—United States. I. Selnow, Gary W. II. Title.
    III. Series.
    Z6951.R55   1989
    [PN4877]
    015.73034—dc20   89-17221

British Library Cataloguing in Publication Data is available.

Copyright © 1989 by Sam G. Riley and Gary W. Selnow

All rights reserved. No portion of this book may be
reproduced, by any process or technique, without the
express written consent of the publisher.

Library of Congress Catalog Card Number: 89-17221
ISBN: 0-313-26839-8
ISSN: 0742-5538

First published in 1989

Greenwood Press, Inc.
88 Post Road West, Westport, Connecticut 06881

Printed in the United States of America

The paper used in this book complies with the
Permanent Paper Standard issued by the National
Information Standards Organization (Z39.48-1984).

10 9 8 7 6 5 4 3 2 1

To all the men and women,
who for whatever reason,
founded a city or regional magazine.

Contents

Acknowledgments

Thanks are given to Marilyn Brownstein of Greenwood Press for her help in planning this book and its forthcoming companion volume, Regional Interest Magazines of the United States, which will provide analytical essays and additional documentation on selective magazines. We are especially grateful to the reference staff of the Newman Library at Virginia Polytechnic Institute and State University for their help and cooperation in the gathering of information for these listings. Heartfelt thanks are also extended to Norma Montgomery of the VPI & SU Communication Studies staff for her ever cheerful help in word processing.

INDEX TO
CITY AND REGIONAL
MAGAZINES
OF THE
UNITED STATES

Introduction

Regional and city magazines have constituted one of the most dynamic sectors of the United States magazine industry since shortly after World War II, the period in which mass circulation magazines began to lose ground to more specialized periodicals. In the vibrant post-WW II market many new magazines specialized by subject matter; others sought their market niche through geographic identification, following the lead of such successful earlier titles as Sunset (1898), New Yorker (1923), and Yankee (1935) that capitalized on close association with region or city.

Replacing or competing with the unabashedly commercial, mercantile chamber of commerce magazines in major U.S. cities were such new arrivals as San Diego (1948); Chicago (1952), which began as a program guide for station WFMT; Los Angeles (1960); Boston Magazine (1962); Washingtonian (1965); New York Magazine (1968), originally a supplement to the New York Herald Tribune; and Philadelphia, which had begun as a chamber periodical in 1908 and converted to independent status in 1964. These magazines were slick, attractively laid out, full of color, and more dependent on service journalism than on literary content. The same can be said of post-WW II regionals such as Vermont Life (1946), Southern Living (1966), and Texas Monthly (1973). Soon these new magazines were fat with ads, and publishers in smaller markets set out to emulate their success.

Most of the new city magazines were "urban survival manuals" for the relatively affluent--guides to the best shopping, the best dining, the best entertainment that a city had to offer. Some retained the "never is said a discouraging word" tone of their chamber of commerce predecessors; others, most notably Philadelphia, Boston Magazine and Washingtonian, also ran hard-hitting investigative pieces. Among the regionals, titles such as Vermont Life, Yankee and Southern Living have traded nicely on the attractions of quasi-nostalgic regional mystique. Texas Monthly was more frankly journalistic and soon made a national reputation for muckraking Texas style, as well as for its living writing. All, however, were filling a service need: acquainting residents, newcomers and visitors with the how-to, where-to, and when-to of modern living, as well as providing interpretative articles on various close-to-home issues and profiles of prominent players on the local or regional scene.

All too often writers commenting on the explosive growth of city and regional magazines after World War II make it sound as though geographic specialization was something entirely new to this period.   While this genre of service-oriented niche magazines is indeed largely a post-WW II creation, American magazines that chose to identify themselves geographically have been around since the 1743 appearance of America's third magazine, the Boston Weekly Magazine.   Some early magazines that appended their city's name to their titles were probably doing no more than following the precedent of newspapers, which have usually identified themselves by city in their nameplates.   Others seem to have included their city's name in their titles in order to write about and capitalize on that which was distinctive, or even unique to their community.

Prior to the mid-1800s, the vast majority of all U.S. magazines were either local or regional in circulation.   Only a handful of titles had national circulation of any size, and even magazines having the words "U.S." or "American" or "National" in their titles were simply unable to achieve substantial circulation outside their own locales.   Clearly the Civil War had the effect of intensifying this localism.

Later in the 1800s a few "booster magazines" appeared and joined newspapers in extolling the virtues of their locale in an attempt to attract economic development.   Examples are Northwest Magazine (1883-1903) and Virginias (1880-1885).   It can safely be said, however, that even as recently as the 1940s, most magazines of general circulation that identified themselves geographically were more literary in their aims than they were service-oriented, and less concerned with their readers' use of leisure time and extra cash.

In an attempt to provide historical perspective for today's city and regional magazines, we offer in Appendix A an alphabetical listing of magazines that identified themselves geographically and that published and perished prior to 1950.   The list is far from complete, but is representative.   Each entry shows title, city and state of publication, dates of publication, and title changes, if known.

This book's main emphasis is on regional interest magazines that have been in existence between 1950 and 1988.   We were able to locate 920 such magazines; these magazines were listed alphabetically by title in Part I.   Entries also include city and state of publication, years of publication (open-ended if still being published in 1988, e.g., 1970 -), type of magazine (designated by number as explained below), and frequency of publication (1=weekly, 2=monthly, 3=bimonthly, 4=quarterly, 5=other).   Online Computer Library Center (OCLC) symbols indicate known library holdings; a list of these symbols, arranged by state, appears in Appendix B.

Part II lists titles only, arranged chronologically by year founded. Part III lists titles geographically by state, then alphabetically within each state.

Sources most useful in compiling this listing were the Gale (formerly Ayer) Directory of Publications, the Standard Periodical Directory, Ulrich's International Periodicals Directory, Standard Rate and Data Service Inc.'s Consumer Magazine & Agri-Media Rates & Data, the Union List of Serials, Writer's Market, the OCLC electronic database, and Folio, the trade magazine of the magazine industry.

The reader should be aware that choice of terminology poses a problem in describing these magazines. The term "city magazine" has been used by several earlier writers and by the editors of Time to describe not only New York, Washingtonian and Atlanta, but such magazines as Texas Monthly or Vermont Life, which have statewide appeal, and even Sunset or Southern Living, magazines whose specialized geographical appeal is to a much larger region. By the same token, other writers have used the term "metropolitan magazine" to refer to all periodicals that specialize by city (Chicago), part of a state (North Carolina's short-lived New East), state (Louisiana Life), parts of several states (Mid-Atlantic Country), or an even larger geographical region (Yankee).

Still others, including the useful reference book Writer's Market, have preferred to use the more encompassing term "regional magazine" to cover all these periodicals--a preferable designation but still not entirely satisfactory inasmuch as San Diego or D (the city magazine of Dallas, Texas) are more nearly geared to city than to region.

In his book American Magazines for the 1980s, William H. Taft includes a chapter titled "City, State and Regional Magazines." Though this designation would seem to cover all the bases, it really doesn't quite do so, as it offers no term to describe yet another important variety of geographically identified magazines: those that specialize not only by descriptive coverage of the city, state, or region in which they are published, but by some particular subject matter as well. Examples are Austin Homes & Gardens, a city house book; Wildlife in North Carolina, covering that state's animal life and related nature topics; Windy City Sports, on Chicago's sports scene; and Virginia Cavalcade, a state magazine of popular history.

In his book Magazines for Millions, James L. Ford has expressed misgivings over using "city magazine" to refer even to such titles as Chicago or Philadelphia or Honolulu because their real editorial emphasis is as much on suburban as on urban interests. Professor Gene Burd of the University of Texas validly points out that most "city magazines" contain articles of wider regional interest in addition to those more narrowly focused on the city proper. All in all, then, no system of terminology for these magazines would appear likely to satisfy everyone.

In the view of the present authors, the most appropriate umbrella term to cover all these geographically identified magazines is the one used by the Standard Periodical Directory: regional interest magazines. This designation has enough latitude to encompass all the periodicals included in this study.

The authors have taken a broad view of these regional interest magazines and have employed four designations for purposes of classifying general consumer interest magazines that identify themselves geographically, either by title, which is usually the case, or by editorial content, as with Town Topics of New York City; Bittersweet of Cornish, Maine; or Ohio's Bend of the River Magazine. The four designations of magazine type we have used are as follows:

1. City Magazine--magazines such as Cleveland Magazine, Las Vegan, Nashville!, or Philadelphia Magazine that devote their predominant

editorial interest to articles in a considerable variety of subject areas, all of which are tied to the city and its immediate surrounds.

2.   Regional Magazine--those periodicals of varied editorial content that are geared mainly to a state, part of a state, parts of more than one state, more than a single state, or a larger geographical region such as the South or the Northwest.

3.   City Specialty Magazine--consumer magazines that, like <u>Albuquerque Senior Scene Magazine</u>, <u>Atlanta Skier</u>, <u>Houston Home & Garden</u>, or <u>Hartford Woman</u>, specialize not only geographically by city, but also by a particular subject matter (sports, house and garden interests, women's issues, and the like).

4.   Regional Specialty Magazine--those that specialize geographically by something broader than city interest and, in addition, specialize by subject content: <u>California Homes and Lifestyles</u>, <u>Carolina Game and Fish</u>, <u>Colorado Outdoor Journal</u>, <u>Great Lakes Sailor</u>, or <u>Southern Homes</u>.

Varieties of periodicals <u>not</u> included in this study are newspaper magazine sections, airline inflight magazines, city or regional business magazines, regionally oriented farm magazines, college or university alumni magazines, education periodicals, city and regional church periodicals, motor club periodicals (with the exception of a few of the biggest and best of these), regional academic and professional journals, and any other periodicals not read by a relatively general consumer audience. In addition, any periodical known to be published as an annual or in tabloid format was excluded, as were city guides that lack substantial editorial content.

Table 1 shows the number of regional interest periodicals we were able to locate that were published during the period 1950-1988 in each state and the District of Columbia and each state's percentage of the total.   California leads the nation in the production of these magazines, with a total of 91.   It is not surprising that our other most populous states follow: New York with 78, Texas with 70, and Florida with 69.

Other states especially productive of regional interest magazines are Georgia (41), Virginia (33), Illinois (31), and with 30 each, Massachusetts, Michigan and Pennsylvania.   Still other states that have produced more than 20 such magazines since 1950 are Colorado (23), Ohio (22), and Connecticut (21).

At the low end of the frequency spectrum, we were unable to locate any regional type magazines published in South Dakota.   States having had but two such magazines are Delaware and Wyoming; those with three each are North Dakota and Rhode Island.   Nevada and West Virginia have had four each, and Iowa, Nebraska, and the District of Columbia have each had five.

Table 1 Regional publications by state

Value	Frequency	Percent	Valid Percent
AK	8	.9	.9
AL	10	1.1	1.1
AR	9	1.0	1.0
AZ	19	2.1	2.1
CA	91	9.9	9.9
CO	23	2.5	2.5
CT	21	2.3	2.3
DC	5	.5	.5
DE	2	.2	.2
FL	69	7.5	7.5
GA	41	4.5	4.5
HI	12	1.3	1.3
IA	5	.5	.5
ID	8	.9	.9
IL	31	3.4	3.4
IN	12	1.3	1.3
KS	6	.7	.7
KY	10	1.1	1.1
LA	15	1.6	1.6
MA	30	3.3	3.3
MD	7	.8	.8
ME	10	1.1	1.1
MI	30	3.3	3.3
MN	8	.9	.9
MO	17	1.8	1.8
MS	7	.8	.8
MT	8	.9	.9
NB	2	.2	.2
NC	19	2.1	2.1
ND	3	.3	.3
NE	3	.3	.3
NH	9	1.0	1.0
NJ	17	1.8	1.8
NM	10	1.1	1.1
NV	4	.4	.4
NY	78	8.5	8.5
OH	22	2.4	2.4
OK	8	.9	.9
OR	11	1.2	1.2
PA	30	3.3	3.3
RI	3	.3	.3
SC	16	1.7	1.7
TN	11	1.2	1.2
TX	70	7.6	7.6
UT	8	.9	.9
VA	33	3.6	3.6
VT	11	1.2	1.2
WA	15	1.6	1.6
WI	16	1.7	1.7
WV	4	.4	.4
WY	2	.2	.2
Total	920	100.0	100.0

Looking at 1950-1988 regional interest magazines by type, 40% have been regional magazines, 29% city magazines, 22% regional specialty magazines, and slightly less then 6% city specialty magazines. See Table 2 below.

Table 2   Regional Interest Magazines by type

	Number	Percent
Regional	371	40.3
City	267	29.0
Regional Specialty	206	22.4
City Specialty	52	5.7
Missing Cases	24	2.6
	920	100.0

In frequency of publication, 51% of these magazines are monthlies, 21% bimonthlies, 11% quarterlies, 2% weeklies, and 10% other. See Table 3.

Table 3   Regional Interest Magazines by frequency of publication

	Number	Percent
Monthly	472	51.3
Bimonthly	190	20.7
Quarterly	100	10.9
Weekly	17	1.8
Other	92	10.0
Missing Cases	49	5.3
	920	100.0

The number of regional magazine start-ups has increased with each passing decade since the 1950s. Of all the regional magazines that have been in publication between 1950 and 1988, only 29 were started from 1900 to 1929. Thirty-one were started during the 1930s, and 41 during the 1940s. The number of magazine start-ups nearly doubled to 78 during the 1950s. As Table 4 shows, the number of starts during the 1960s, 127, was considerably more impressive. Of all the U.S. regional magazines published since 1950, more than 50 percent began after 1970. The 1980s, with 271 regional magazines started as of the end of 1988, will no doubt outpace all other periods. With advancement of desk top publishing technology, it is likely that the years upcoming will offer even greater opportunities for publishers to tap regional markets. See Table 4 for a breakdown of magazine starts.

Table 4   Regional magazine start up dates during the 1900s.
(For magazines in publication between 1950 and 1988)

	Number	Percent	Valid Percent
1900-1929	29	3.2	3.4
1930-1939	31	3.4	3.6
1940-1949	41	4.5	4.8
1950-1959	78	8.5	9.1
1960-1969	127	13.8	14.8
1970-1979	280	30.4	32.7
1980-1988	271	29.5	31.6
Unknown starts	63	6.8	missing

While the number of starts has increased throughout the 1900s there is reasonable consistency in the types of regionals begun during each decade. As Table 5 shows, of all magazine types started in each ten year period, roughly a quarter to a third were city magazines, and about a quarter were regional specialty types. Of these magazines begun in the '50s there was a slightly greater proportion of regional types than there were in the '80s; these differences are not startling. As compared to previous periods, a greater portion of regional interest magazines started during the '80s were of the city specialty type. This suggests a slight tendency for recent regional interest magazine publishers to give more emphasis to the city specialty variety than was the case before. This would be expected: Not only are regional magazines now focusing on readers within a geographic region, but, increasingly, on special interest areas as well. This is a demonstration of the ever more refined audiences targeted by regional magazine publishers.

Table 5   Magazine type by decade magazine started publication

	< 1950		1950-59		1960-69		1970-79		1980-87	
	n	%	n	%	n	%	n	%	n	%
City	49	31.8	18	25.0	39	32.2	90	32.3	66	26.3
Regl	56	36.4	34	47.2	50	41.3	125	44.8	96	38.2
City Spec	3	1.9	2	2.8	1	.8	12	4.3	33	13.1
Regl Spec	46	29.9	18	25.0	31	25.6	52	18.6	56	22.3

There is considerable variance in the longevity of regional magazines. As might be expected, according to this data, some never last beyond their first year. Others, however, have remained in production some 90 years. The average longevity of this collection is nearly 17 years (16.6 years). Table 6 provides, roughly, a quartile split according to longevity. The reader should note that all magazines are represented in this table including those started as late as 1988. Naturally recent entrants still in publication tend to make the longevity of regionals appear a bit more dire than is actually the case. These statistics, then, are for magazines that have terminated as well as those still in production.

Table 6   Longevity of Regional Magazines

	n	Percent	Valid Percent
4 years and less	152	16.5	24.8
5 to 10 years	156	16.9	25.4
11 to 21 years	150	16.3	24.5
More than 22 years	155	16.9	25.4
Unknown	307	33.4	missing

There are several differences in the frequency of publication by magazine type (see Table 7). Generally, city and city specialty magazines tend to publish more frequently than do regional and regional specialty types. Well over half the city magazines publish on a monthly schedule, while fewer than half of the regional types do so. Regionals are more likely to publish bimonthly or quarterly. It appears, then, that as these magazines become more focused geographically and by interest category, they also tend to appear more often. They are more focused in appeal and more frequent in delivery of information.

Table 7   Frequency by type of magazine

Type	City		Regional		Cty Spec		Reg Spec	
	n	%	n	%	n	%	n	%
Weekly	6	2.4	6	1.7	2	4.1	2	1.0
Monthly	167	67.1	175	48.6	28	57.1	88	45.8
Bi-monthly	39	15.7	89	24.7	7	14.3	51	26.6
Quarterly	18	7.2	54	15.0	3	6.1	24	12.5
Other	19	7.6	36	10.0	9	18.4	27	14.1

Two noteworthy observations emerge from the data collected in this study. First, there have been a greater number of regional maga nes started during recent years than ever before. This follows a general media trend, which has seen the numbers of nearly all broadcast and print outlets increase considerably since the 1950s. There is a general trend for a greater number and variety of media as each is designed to appeal to ever more narrow and focused audiences.

A case can be made for an increased targeting of regional maga- zines. Although this study did not examine content of these publications, it appears reasonable to assume that as a greater number of regional magazines appear, each must carve for itself a piece of the market or an audience block to which it can focus its editorial and advertising content. This case also is made in recent years by a measurable increase in the proportion of city specialty magazines. Such publications focus on narrow geographic and audience interest characteristics. This is the es- sence of most targeted media strategies.

Second, it is evident from these figures that the most focused re- gional magazines also are publishing with greatest frequency. The ma- jority of city and city specialty publications appear monthly while the majority of regional and regional specialty magazines publish on a bi- monthly or quarterly basis. If this trend holds up, as regional magazines become more focused we may anticipate a greater publication frequency as well.

The accessibility of desk top publishing equipment likely will affect regional magazines. Typesetting and production costs, once an impediment for many would-be publishers, now have been reduced substantially by emerging technologies. A regional magazine can get off the ground with only modest funding, a few good ideas, and just a handful of readers. Although many such starts likely will not meet with commercial success, recent trends suggest the market for regional specialty magazines is growing and the public can support a sizable number of publications. There is every reason to expect, based on data gathered in this study and on the implications of advances in publication technology, that regional magazines will grow in their importance to the American media repertoire.

Part I

Alphabetical List of Regional Interest Magazines, 1950-1988 (Arranged by date founded)

A P T   (Austin People Today)
Austin   TX
1971 - Unkwn
Type: 1 Frequency: 2

Above the Bridge Magazine
Gwinn   MI
1985 -
Type: 2 Frequency: Unkwn
EEX, EZT

*Acadiana Profile; A Magazine for
Bi-lingual Louisiana*
Lafayette   LA
1969 -
Type: 4 Frequency: 3
AKC, DLC, CEN, LLM, LNC, LUU

Accent West
Amarillo   TX
1972 -
Type: 2 Frequency: 2
OKN, TAP, TWT

Adirondack Life
Jay   NY
1970 -
Type: 2 Frequency: 3
DLC

Alabama Game & Fish
Marietta   GA
1980 -
Type: 4 Frequency: 2
AAA, AMP

Alabama Magazine
Montgomery   AL
1936 -
Type: 2 Frequency: 2
AAA, ABC, CFI, NOC, TJC

Alabama Monthly
Tuscaloosa   AL
1980 - 1981
Type: 2 Frequency: 3
Earlier Title: Alabama Living
AAA, ALM

Alaska Geographic
Anchorage   AK
1972 -
Type: 4 Frequency: 4
DLC, NJB, TCN, VPI

Alaska Journal
Anchorage   AK
1971 -
Type: 2 Frequency: 4
DLC, TKN, VA@, VPI

Alaska Magazine
Anchorage   AK
1969 -
Type: 2 Frequency: 2
AZT, CLB, DLC, GUA, HUH, VWM

Alaska Outdoors
Anchorage   AK
1978 -
Type: 4 Frequency: 3
OXY

Alaska Woman
Anchorage   AK
1982 -
Type: 4 Frequency: 2

*Alaska; Magazine of Life on the
Last Frontier*
Anchorage   AK
1935 -
Type: 2 Frequency: 2
Earlier Title: Alaska Sportsman
CUR, CUT, IXA, OKU, YUS

*Albuquerque Senior Scene Maga-
zine*
Albuquerque   NM
1987 -
Type: 3 Frequency: 4

Alburquerque Singles Magazine
Alburquerque   NM
1976 -
Type: 3 Frequency: 2

All Florida Magazine
Jacksonville   FL
Unkwn - Unkwn
Type: 2 Frequency: 1
ORL

*Aloha, The Magazine of Hawaii and
the Pacific*
Honolulu   HI
1977 -
Type: 2 Frequency: 3
HIL, HUH

American West
Tucson   AZ
1964 -
Type: 2 Frequency: 3
AZU, CBA, BHU, FDA, IAO, IXA

Angeles
Los Angeles   CA
1988
Type: 1 Frequency: 2

Ann Arbor Observer
Ann Arbor   MI
1976 -
Type: 1 Frequency: 2
EEX, EYA

Ann Arbor Scene Magazine
Ann Arbor   MI
1972 -
Type: 1 Frequency: 4
EEX, EHL

Appalachian Heritage
Berea   KY
1973 -
Type: 2 Frequency:.4
DLC, KBE, NJB, TKL, VA@, VPI

Arizona Arts & Travel
Paradise Valley AZ
1983 -
Type: 4 Frequency: 5
ATM, AZT, AZU

Arizona Golf Journal
Scottsdale   AZ
1984 -
Type: 4 Frequency: 3
ATM

Arizona Highways
Phoenix   AZ
1925 -
Type: 2 Frequency: 2
PNX, CGN, COF, DLC, IAA

Arizona Living
Phoenix   AZ
1970 -
Type: 2 Frequency: 2
ATM, AZN, AZS, AZT

Arizona Monthly
Phoeniz   AZ
1987 -
Type: 2 Frequency: 5
MSA

Arizona Wildlife Sportsman
Phoenix   AZ
1928 - 1955
Type: 4 Frequency: 2
AZH, AZS, AZU, YAM

Ark/Ozark
Eureka Springs AR
1968 - Unkwn
Type: 2 Frequency: 4
AKU

Arkansan
Little Rock   AR
1979 - 1980
Type: 2 Frequency: 2
AFU, AKC, AKU, DLC

Arkansas Fisherman
Little Rock   AR
1979 - Unkwn
Type: 4 Frequency: 2

Arkansas Sportsman
Marietta   GA
1946 -
Type: 4 Frequency: 2
DLC

Arkansas State Magazine
Little Rock   AR
1966 - 1967
Type: 2 Frequency: 4
AFU, AKC, AKH, AKU

Arkansas Times
Little Rock   AR
1974 -
Type: 2 Frequency: 2
AFU, AKC

Atlanta Arts
Atlanta   GA
1968 - Unkwn
Type: 4 Frequency: 2
DLC, GUA, IUL

Atlanta Impressions
Atlanta   GA
1981 - Unkwn
Type: 1 Frequency: 4
DLC, GUA

Atlanta Magazine
Atlanta   GA
1961 -
Type: 1 Frequency: 2
FDA, IBA, TKN

Atlanta Singles Magazine &
Datebook
Atlanta   GA
1977 -
Type: 3 Frequency: 2

Atlanta Skier
Atlanta   GA
1967 -
Type: 3 Frequency: 4
GUA

Atlantic City Express
New York   NY
1981 - Unkwn
Type: 1 Frequency: 2

Atlantic City Magazine
Atlantic City   NJ
1977 -
Type: 1 Frequency: 2
ACN, CMP, NCL, NJL, NJR

Atlantic City Night Life
Deer Park   NY
1984 - Unkwn
Type: 3 Frequency: 2

Atlantic Coastal Diver
Baltimore   MD
Unkwn - Unkwn
Type: 4 Frequency: 3

Augusta Magazine
Augusta   GA
1966 -
Type: 1 Frequency: 3
GJG, GUA, GXM

Augusta Spectator
Augusta   GA
1980 -
Type: 1 Frequency: 5

Austin Arts & Leisure
Austin   TX
1979 - Unkwn
Type: 3 Frequency: Unkwn
IXA

Austin Homes & Gardens
Austin   TX
1980 -
Type: 3 Frequency: 2

Austin Living
Austin   TX
1974 -
Type: 1 Frequency: 3
IXA, IYU

Austin Magazine
Austin   TX
1960 -
Type: 1 Frequency: 5
IGA, ILU, IXA, TXA, TXN

Austin People Today
Austin   TX
1971 - Unkwn
Type: 1 Frequency: 2

Austin Woman
Austin   TX
1983 -
Type: 3 Frequency: 5
IWU, IXA, IYU, TXG, TXQ

Avenue
New York   NY
1976 -
Type: 1 Frequency: 2

Avenue M
Chicago   IL
1975 -
Type: 1 Frequency: 2

Back Home in Kentucky
Mt Morris   KY
1977 -
Type: 2 Frequency: 3

Bakersfield Lifestyle Magazine
Bakersfield   CA
1981 -
Type: 1 Frequency: 2

Baltimore Magazine
Baltimore   MD
1906 -
Type: 1 Frequency: 2
CRL, BAL

Baltimore Scene
Baltimore   MD
1963 -
Type: 1 Frequency: 3

Bay Life Magazine
Tampa   FL
1978 - 1980
Type: 2 Frequency: 2
FHM, FUG

*Bay Views; Reflecting the Good
Life of the Golden Gate*
San Rafael   CA
1977 - Unkwn
Type: 1 Frequency: 2

Bay Window
Newport Beach   CA
1951 -
Type: 1 Frequency: 2

Beacon Magazine of Hawaii
Honolulu   HI
1957 - 1975
Type: 2 Frequency: 2

Bend of the River Magazine
Perrysburg   OH
1972 -
Type: 4 Frequency: 2
EHL, BGU, TOL, WIH

Beverly Hills
Beverly Hills   CA
1983 -
Type: 1 Frequency: 1
LPU

Beverly Hills World
Los Angeles   CA
1982 - Unkwn
Type: 1 Frequency: 5
LPU

*Big Valley, The San Fernando
Valley Magazine*
Sapulveda   CA
Unkwn -
Type: 2 Frequency: 2
CNO, LPU

Birmingham
Birmingham   AL
1961 -
Type: 1 Frequency: 2
ALM

*Bittersweet, The Flavor of
Northcountry Living*
Cornish   ME
Unkwn - Unkwn
Type: Unkwn Frequency: 5

Black New Orleans
New Orleans   LA
1982 - Unkwn
Type: 3 Frequency: 2
LDA, LNU, LRU

Blair & Ketchum's Country Journal
Manchester   VT
1974 -
Type: 2 Frequency: 2
DLC, NPC, TNN, VPI, WVU

Blue Ridge Country
Roanoke   VA
1988
Type: 3 Frequency: 3

Blvd
Kansas City   MO
1982 - Unkwn
Type: 1 Frequency: 2

Boat Pennsylvania
Harrisburg   PA
1984 -
Type: 4 Frequency: 4
NYG, DKC, PBU, PIT

Boca Raton Magazine
Boca Raton   FL
1981 -
Type: 1 Frequency: 3
FGM

Borrowed Times
Missoula   MT
1972 - 1979
Type: 4 Frequency: 1
AZS, CDS, KSU, OKX

Boston
Boston   MA
1954 - 1962
Type: 1 Frequency: Unkwn
MAS

Boston Magazine
Boston   MA
1962 -
Type: 1 Frequency: 2
BET, HLS, SUF, NHM, TKN

Boston Monthly, The
Boston   MA
1979 -
Type: 1 Frequency: 2
UCW

Boston Woman
Boston   MA
1986 -
Type: 3 Frequency: 2
CPY, DHP, SCL

Bostonia, The Magazine of Culture & Ideas
Brookline   MA
1900 -
Type: Unkwn Frequency: 3
DLC, BOS, MBU, WAY

Boulevards, The Magazine of San Francisco
San Francisco   CA
1981 - 1989
Type: 1 Frequency: 2
WIH

Bronx Westchester Life
New York   NY
1950 - Unkwn
Type: 2 Frequency: 2

Broome County Living
Binghamton   NY
1975 -
Type: 2 Frequency: 2
COO, YTR

Broward Life
Ft Lauderdale FL
1974 - 1981
Type: 2 Frequency: 5
Earlier Title: Gold Coast of Florida
EDB, NYP

Brown Texan
Fort Worth   TX
1964 - Unkwn
Type: 4 Frequency: 2

Brown's Guide to Georgia
College Park   GA
1972 - 1982
Type: 2 Frequency: 5
EMU, GAP, GAS, GSU, GUA

Bucks County Life
Doylestown   PA
1960 - 1968
Type: 2 Frequency: 2
TFP, BUC, PLF

Bucks County Panorama Magazine
Doylestown   PA
1958 - 1978
Type: 2 Frequency: 2
TFP, BUC, PIT, SRS

Buffalo
Buffalo   NY
1933 - 1963
Type: 1 Frequency: 2

Buffalo Scene Magazine
Buffalo   NY
1984 - Unkwn
Type: 3 Frequency: 2
ILS, BUF, VKC, VVH

Buffalo Spree Magazine
Buffalo   NY
1967 - Unkwn
Type: 2 Frequency: 4

BFLO
Buffalo   NY
1974 - Unkwn
Type: 2 Frequency: 5

California
Los Angeles   CA
1976 -
Type: 2 Frequency: 2
Earlier Title: New West
AZU, CSF, HUH

California & Western Visitor
Los Angeles   CA
1954 - Unkwn
Type: 2 Frequency: 2

California Angler
Carlsbad   CA
1981 -
Type: 4 Frequency: 5
Earlier Title: Western Saltwater
Fisherman
DLC, WAC

California Basketball
Redondo Beach   CA
1988
Type: 4 Frequency: Unkwn

California Homes and Lifestyles
Costa Mesa   CA
1983 -
Type: 4 Frequency: 4
Earlier Title: California Homes

California Journal
Sacramento   CA
1970 -
Type: 4 Frequency: 2
CSA, SMP

Californian
San Francisco   CA
1960 - 1965
Type: 2 Frequency: 2
CLU, MUL N, YP

Cape Cod Compass
Chatham   MA
1949 -
Type: 2 Frequency: 5
CZL, CXM Y, QR VA, @

Cape Cod Guide
Plymouth   MA
1946 -
Type: 2 Frequency: 1

Cape Cod Life
Osterville   MD
1979 -
Type: 2 Frequency: 3
GME, WHP, CXD, ABR, NYP

Capital Magazine
Falls Church   VA
1974 -
Type: 1 Frequency: Unkwn

Capital Region Magazine
Albany   NY
1985 -
Type: 2 Frequency: 2
NAM, NYG, VKM, VTU

*Capital Shopper: The Magazine
That Pays for Itself*
Fairfax   VA
1980 - Unkwn
Type: 3 Frequency: Unkwn
FTC

Carolina Game and Fish
Marietta   GA
1981 -
Type: 4 Frequency: 2

Carolina Golfer
Charlotte   NC
1960 - Unkwn
Type: 4 Frequency: Unkwn
SGR

Carolina Lifestyle
Norfolk   VA
1982 - 1983
Type: 2 Frequency: 5
NCS, NDD, NGU, TNS, VIC

Carolina Sportsman
Charlotte   NC
1960 - Unkwn
Type: 4 Frequency: Unkwn
NRC

Cascades East
Bend   OR
1976 -
Type: 2 Frequency: 4
CEO, DCH, ORU

Center Magazine
Louisville   KY
1983 -
Type: 4 Frequency: 2
Earlier Title: Kentucky Premier
Magazine

Central Florida Magazine
Orlando   FL
1973 -
Type: 2 Frequency: 2
Earlier Title: Central Florida
Scene
FUG

Central New Yorker
Syracuse   NY
1961 -
Type: 2 Frequency: 2

Champaign-Urbana Magazine
Champaign   IL
1981 -
Type: 1 Frequency: 2

Charleston Magazine
Charleston   SC
1975 - Unkwn
Type: 1 Frequency: 2
MUL, NYP, SBM, SXC, IXA

Charlotte Magazine
Charlotte   NC
1968 -
Type: 1 Frequency: 2
NKM, NNM

Charlotte Metrolina Magazine
Charlotte   NC
1968 - 1970
Type: 1 Frequency: 3
NKM, NNM

Chesapeake Bay Magazine
Annapolis   MD
1971 -
Type: 2 Frequency: 2
DGW, MDS, MFS, PHA, VPL

Chicago
Chicago   IL
1952 -
Type: 1 Frequency: 2
CGP, IAL, IBV, VWM

Chicago Guide
Chicago   IL
1952 - 1974
Type: 1 Frequency: 2
CGP, IAC, IAF, COO, EEM

Chicago History
Chicago   IL
1945 -
Type: 3 Frequency: 4
CGP, IBZ, SVP

Chicago Independent Magazine
Chicago   IL
1975 - Unkwn
Type: 3 Frequency: 2

Chicago Life
Chicago   IL
1984 -
Type: 1 Frequency: 2

Chicago Mahogany
Harvey   IL
1980 - Unkwn
Type: 3 Frequency: 2

Chicago Omnibus
Chicago   IL
Unkwn - Unkwn
Type: 1 Frequency: Unkwn

Chicago Reporter, The
Chicago   IL
1972 -
Type: 3 Frequency: 2
DLC, CGP, IAC, IBZ, TXT

Chicago Scene
Chicago   IL
1960 - Unkwn
Type: 1 Frequency: 2
CGP, IAL, IAO, IUL

Chicago Sports Scene
Elk Grove Vill   IL
1980 - 1982
Type: 3 Frequency: 2
CGP, ICG

Chicago Times
Chicago   IL
1987 -
Type: 1 Frequency: 3

Chicagoan
Chicago   IL
1973 - 1974
Type: 1 Frequency: 2
DLC, CGP, IAA, IUL, NYP

Chicagoland
Chicago   IL
Unkwn - Unkwn
Type: 1 Frequency: Unkwn

Chronicles of Oklahoma, The
Oklahoma City   OK
1921 -
Type: 4 Frequency: Unkwn
RRR, ZXC, OKX

Cincinnati Magazine
Cincinnati   OH
1967 -
Type: 1 Frequency: 2
Earlier Title: Cincinnati Monthly
DLC, NYP, CHT, CIN, CLE

City
Kansas City   MO
1978 - Unkwn
Type: 1 Frequency: 2
NYP

City Guide, Broadway Magazine
New York   NY
1982 -
Type: 1 Frequency: 1
Earlier Title: Broadway Magazine

City Limits
Boston   MA
1981 - Unkwn
Type: 1 Frequency: 2

City Limits, News for the the Other New York
New York   NY
Unkwn -
Type: 1 Frequency: 2

City Magazine
San Francisco   CA
1967 - Unkwn
Type: 1 Frequency: 1

City Magazine
Detroit   MI
Unkwn - Unkwn
Type: 1 Frequency: 2
PNX, CUZ, IXA

City Magazine
Rochester   NY
1974
Type: 1 Frequency: 3
RRR, YQR

City-County Magazine
Burlington   NC
1986 -
Type: 4 Frequency: 2

Cleveland Magazine
Cleveland   OH
1972 -
Type: 1 Frequency: 2
DLC, LNC, UMI, NYP, CSU, CLE

Coast & County
Swampscott   MA
1984 -
Type: 2 Frequency: 3
Earlier Title: Lynn; The North Shore Magazine

Coast Magazine
Los Angeles   CA
1960 - Unkwn
Type: 2 Frequency: 2
Earlier Title: Coast FM & Fine Arts

Coast Magazine
Coos Bay   OR
1978 - 1979
Type: 2 Frequency: Unkwn

Coast Magazine
Myrtle Beach   SC
1954 -
Type: 2 Frequency: 1

Coastal Journal
Jaffrey   NH
1983 -
Type: 2 Frequency: 4
CTW, MAS

Coastal Magazine
Savannah   GA
1975 - 1978
Type: 2 Frequency: 3
Earlier Title: Coastal Quarterly
GPM

Coastline Magazine
Culver City   CA
1973 - Unkwn
Type: 2 Frequency: 3

Cola. The Magazine of Columbia
Columbia   SC
Present
Type: 1 Frequency: 4

Colorado Art Scene
Denver   CO
1983 - Unkwn
Type: 4 Frequency: 4

Colorado Express, The
Denver   CO
1972 -
Type: 3 Frequency: 5
COA, COF, COS, CGP, PHA

Colorado Homes & Lifestyles
Denver   CO
1980 -
Type: 4 Frequency: 3
COA, DLC, WYU

Colorado Magazine
Denver   CO
1966 - 1978
Type: 2 Frequency: 4
MWR, MSA, CLO, CDF, COF, VPI

Colorado Outdoor Journal
Florence   CO
1986 -
Type: 4 Frequency: 3

Colorado Outdoors
Denver   CO
1952 -
Type: 4 Frequency: 3
DNH, LDL

Colorado Sports Monthly
Colorado Sprin   CO
1980 -
Type: 4 Frequency: 3
DPL

Colorado Sportstyles Magazine
Terrance   CA
1979 -
Type: 4 Frequency: 2
DPL

Colorado Springs Monthly
Colorado Spring CO
1979 - Unkwn
Type: 1 Frequency: 2

Colorado Woman
Denver   CO
1976 - 1977
Type: 4 Frequency: 3
COA, COG, DPL

Colorado Wonderland
Colorado Sprin   CO
1949 - Unkwn
Type: 2 Frequency: 3
LPU, COG, DPL, UUM, WYU

Colorado/Rocky Mountain West
Denver   CO
1966 - 1980
Type: 2 Frequency: 5
Earlier Title: Rocky Mountain
Magazine
OKX

Colorful Colorado
Denver   CO
1965 - Unkwn
Type: 2 Frequency: 4
JNA, BGU

Columbia Review
Columbia   SC
1983 -
Type: 1 Frequency: 2
DLC, SUC

Columbiana
Oroville   WA
1978 -
Type: 2 Frequency: 4

Columbus Homes & Lifestyles
Columbus   OH
1984 - Unkwn
Type: 3 Frequency: 3

Columbus Magazine
Columbus   GA
1982 - Unkwn
Type: Unkwn Frequency: 1
DLC

Columbus Monthly
Columbus   OH
1975 -
Type: 1 Frequency: 2
CLE, OCO, OHI

Commonwealth Magazine
Norfolk   VA
1934 - 1985
Type: 2 Frequency: 2
DLC, IXA, VA@

Connecticut Country Life
City: Unkwn   CT
1985 - Unkwn
Type: 2 Frequency: 2
Earlier Title: Country Home &
Garden

Connecticut Fireside
Hamden   CT
1972 -
Type: 2 Frequency: 4
BPT, GPI, UCW

Connecticut Magazine
Bridgeport   CT
1971 -
Type: 2 Frequency: 2

Connecticut Riding
Hartford   CT
1983
Type: 4 Frequency: 2
GMY

Connecticut Travels
New Haven   CT
1980 -
Type: 2 Frequency: 2

Connecticut's Finest
Knoxville   TN
1985 - Unkwn
Type: 2 Frequency: 4

Coral Springs Monthly
Coral Springs   FL
Unkwn -
Type: 1 Frequency: 2

Corpus Christi Magazine
Corpus Christi TX
1979 -
Type: 1 Frequency: 2
CCA, CDM

Corvallis Magazine
Corvallis   OR
1962 - 1965
Type: 1 Frequency: 4

Country Life Magazine
City: Unkwn   CT
1982 - 1984
Type: 2 Frequency: 5

Country Magazine, The
Mt Penn   PA
1975 - 1978
Type: 2 Frequency: 2

County Lines
West Chester   PA
1978 -
Type: 2 Frequency: 2
PSC

Cue/New York
New York   NY
1932 - 1980
Type: 1 Frequency: 5
Earlier Title: Cue Magazine
AZN, LPU, GUA, BUF, VHB, ZXC

Cumberland
Clarksville   TN
1977 - Unkwn
Type: 2 Frequency: 2
Earlier Title: Tennessee Monthly
NYP, TNN, TNS

D Magazine
Dallas   TX
1974 -
Type: 1 Frequency: 2
LPU, DLC, BGU, IGA, TXN

Dallas Digest
Dallas   TX
1979 - Unkwn
Type: 1 Frequency: 4

Dallas Magazine
Dallas   TX
1922 -
Type: 1 Frequency: 2
WZW, SDS, IEA, IGA, TXA

Dallas-Fort Worth Home & Garden
Dallas   TX
1978 - 1987
Type: 3 Frequency: 5
LPU, DHU, FUG, IGA, INT

Dallas/Fort Worth Living
Dallas   TX
1972 -
Type: 1 Frequency: 3
IYU

Dayton Magazine
Dayton   OH
1964 -
Type: 1 Frequency: 3
DLC, UMI, CLE, OCP

Dayton USA
Dayton   OH
1964 - Unkwn
Type: 1 Frequency: 3
DLC, IBS, NYP, CLE, IGA

Delaware Monthly
Wilmington   DE
1979
Type: 2 Frequency: 2
DLM

Delaware Today Magazine
Wilmington   DE
1962 - 1983
Type: 2 Frequency: 3
DLC, DLB, DLM, PHA

Delta Review (Jackson)
New York   NY
1958 - Unkwn
Type: Unkwn Frequency: 3

Delta Review (Memphis)
New York   NY
1958 - Unkwn
Type: Unkwn Frequency: 2

Delta Review (New Orleans)
New York   NY
1958 - Unkwn
Type: Unkwn Frequency: 2

Delta Scene
Cleveland   MS
1973 - Unkwn
Type: 2 Frequency: 4
MCD, MFM

Denver
Denver   CO
1970 - 1975
Type: 1 Frequency: 2
DNH, DPL

Denver Living
Denver   CO
1974 - 1983
Type: 1 Frequency: 3
DOA, DPL

Denver Magazine
Denver   CO
1970 -
Type: 1 Frequency: 2
Earlier Title: Denver Singles
Guide
DPL

Denver Monthly
Denver   CO
1972 - 1981
Type: 1 Frequency: 5
Earlier Title: Denver Magazine
COA, DPL, DLC

Desert Magazine
Palm Desert   CA
1968 -
Type: 2 Frequency: 3
IRU

Detroit and Suburban Life
Detroit   MI
Unkwn - Unkwn
Type: 1 Frequency: Unkwn

Detroit Monthly
Detroit   MI
1978 -
Type: 1 Frequency: 2
DLC, EEM, EEX, NYP

Detroit Skyliner
New York   NY
1958 - Unkwn
Type: 1 Frequency: 2

Detroiter, The
Detroit   MI
1977 - Unkwn
Type: 1 Frequency: 2
EEM, EEX

Dimension-Cincinnati
New York   NY
1958 - Unkwn
Type: Unkwn Frequency: 2

Dixie Golf
Atlanta   GA
1967 - Unkwn
Type: 4 Frequency: Unkwn
GUA

Domain
Austin   TX
1987 -
Type: 4 Frequency: 5
IEA, IFA, IUA, TXG

Donde
Miami Beach   FL
1980 -
Type: 2 Frequency: 5

Down East Magazine
Camden   ME
1954 -
Type: 2 Frequency: 2
AZN, DLC, BBH, BYN, MEA

Duluthian, The
Duluth   MN
1924 -
Type: 1 Frequency: 3
MHS, MND, VAP

DM: Des Moines' Metropolitan
Magazine
Des Moines   IA
Unkwn -
Type: 1 Frequency: Unkwn

East End Magazine
Sag Harbor   NY
1979 - Unkwn
Type: 1 Frequency: 2

East-Side Express
New York   NY
1976 - Unkwn
Type: 1 Frequency: 1
NYP

East-West Magazine
Honolulu   HI
1980 -
Type: 2 Frequency: 4
HUH, GZD

Eastern Outdoors
E Lyme   CT
1977 -
Type: 4 Frequency: 3

Eastern Tennis
New York   NY
1960 - Unkwn
Type: 4 Frequency: 4

El Paso Magazine
El Paso   TX
1948 -
Type: 1 Frequency: 2
IXA, IYU, TXU

Elite Magazine, The Southwest
Features/Society Magazine
Scottsdale   AZ
1981 - Unkwn
Type: 2 Frequency: 3

Empire Sports Magazine
Syracuse   NY
1982 - Unkwn
Type: 4 Frequency: 2
XFN, YQR

Empire State Report
Albany   NY
1974 -
Type: 4 Frequency: 2
VYF

Enchantment Magazine
Santa Fe   NM
1950 - Unkwn
Type: 2 Frequency: 2

Erie & Chantauqua Magazine
Erie   PA
1983 -
Type: 2 Frequency: 5
SFM, EPL, UPM

Erie Magazine
Erie   PA
1979 - 1983
Type: 1 Frequency: 5
EPL

Exclusively Yours, Wisconsin
Milwaukee   WI
1947 -
Type: 2 Frequency: 2
GZD

Fairfax
Fairfax   VA
1987 -
Type: 2 Frequency: 2

Fairfield County Magazine
Westport   CT
1954 - 1982
Type: 2 Frequency: 2
Earlier Title: Westchester Magazine

Fairfield County Woman
Stanford   CT
1983 -
Type: 4 Frequency: 2

Faulkner Facts and Fiddlings
Faulkner   AR
1949 -
Type: 4 Frequency: 4
AFU, AKU, AST, DLC

Feather River Territorial
Oroville   CA
1957 - 1961
Type: 2 Frequency: 4
CCH

Fiesta Magazine
McAllen   TX
1970 - Unkwn
Type: 2 Frequency: 2
IYU, TPN

Fishing and Hunting Journal:
Magazine of the Ozark Region
St Louis   MO
1986 -
Type: 4 Frequency: 5
AFU, KUK, SOI

Florida Explorer
Tampa   FL
1952 - Unkwn
Type: 2 Frequency: 2
Earlier Title: Florida Traveler
FUG

Florida Golfer
Miami   FL
1968 - Unkwn
Type: 4 Frequency: 2

Florida Golfweek
Winter Haven   FL
1975 -
Type: 4 Frequency: 3
DLC, FBA, FDA

Florida Gulf Coast Living Magazine
Tampa   FL
1979 -
Type: 2 Frequency: 3

Florida Keys Magazine
Marathan   FL
1978 -
Type: 2 Frequency: 3
DLC

Florida Life
Boca Raton   FL
1973 - Unkwn
Type: 2 Frequency: 2
FDA

Florida Lifestyle
Sanibel   FL
Unkwn -
Type: 2 Frequency: 4

Florida Living
Gainesville   FL
1984 - 1986
Type: 2 Frequency: 2
Earlier Title: North Florida Living
FDA, FUG

Florida Monthly
Miami   FL
1977 -
Type: 2 Frequency: 2

Florida Profile; Sunshine State
Panorama
Ft Lauderdale FL
1966 - Unkwn
Type: 2 Frequency: 4
Earlier Title: Florida Journal
DLC

Florida Sportsman
Miami   FL
1968 -
Type: 4 Frequency: 2
Earlier Title: Gulf Coast Florida
Sportsman
FDA, FHM, FTU

Florida Wildlife
Tallahassee   FL
1947 -
Type: 4 Frequency: 3
AAA, DLC, FDA, FTU, FUG

Florida's Gold Coast
Ft Lauderdale   FL
1965 -
Type: 2 Frequency: 2
Earlier Title: Gold Coast Pictorial
FBR

Focus/Midwest
St Louis   MO
1962 - 1984
Type: 2 Frequency: 3
DLC, KUK, KCP, MUU, NYP

Forest Notes
Concord   NH
1936 -
Type: 4 Frequency: 4
ALM, DRB, NHM, VPI

Fort Collins Magazine
Fort Collins   CO
1977 - Unkwn
Type: 1 Frequency: 3
COF

Fort Wayne
Auburn   IN
Unkwn
Type: 1 Frequency: Unkwn

Four Corner Wonder Land Magazine
Boulder   CO
1962 - Unkwn
Type: 2 Frequency: 5
Earlier Title: Western Gateways
Magazine

Four Corners
Irvington   NJ
1961 - Unkwn
Type: Unkwn Frequency: 2

Frontier; The Voice of the New West
Los Angeles   CA
1949 - 1967
Type: Unkwn Frequency: 3
AZS, AZU, CDS, CSL

Ft Lauderdale Magazine
Ft Lauderdale FL
1962 - Unkwn
Type: 1 Frequency: 3
FGM, FUG

G The Magazine of Gainesville
Gainesville   FL
1982 - Unkwn
Type: 1 Frequency: 5

G, Golden Triad
Greensboro   NC
1978 - Unkwn
Type: 2 Frequency: Unkwn

Galveston Monthly Magazine
Houston   TX
Unkwn -
Type: 1 Frequency: 2

Garden State Home & Garden
Morganville   NJ
1986 -
Type: Unkwn Frequency: 2

Gentry Magazine, The Magazine of Orange County People
Costa Mesa   CA
Unkwn - Unkwn
Type: 2 Frequency: 5

Georgia Journal
Athens   GA
1980 -
Type: 2 Frequency: 4
EMU, GAT, GPM, GUA, NYP

Georgia Life
Decatur   GA
1974 - 1980
Type: 2 Frequency: 5
Earlier Title: Georgia Magazine
GAT, GSU G, UA NY, P

Georgia Magazine
Decatur   GA
1957 - 1973
Type: 2 Frequency: 3
GAT, GSU, NYP

Georgia Outdoors
Atlanta   GA
1962 -
Type: 4 Frequency: 2
GUA, MNP

Georgia Sportsman
Marietta   GA
1976 -
Type: 4 Frequency: 2
GJG, GUA

Gloucester: The Magazine of the New England Coast
Gloucester   MA
1980 -
Type: 1 Frequency: 4
MAS

Golden Gate North
Santa Rosa   CA
1971 - 1973
Type: 2 Frequency: 4

Golden State
San Francisco   CA
1984 -
Type: 2 Frequency: 4
JQW, LPU

Golden West
Freeport   NY
1964 - 1974
Type: 2 Frequency: 3
AZU, DPL, UBY, WYU

Gondolier, Florida's Boating Magazine
1961 - Unkwn
Type: 4 Frequency: Unkwn

Goodlife
Atlanta   GA
1982 -
Type: 2 Frequency: 2
GJG

Grand Rapids Magazine
Grand Rapids   MI
1964 -
Type: 1 Frequency: 2
EEX, EXR, EXW

Grapevine's Finger Lakes Magazine
Ithaca   NY
1985 -
Type: 2 Frequency: 3

Great Lakelands, The
Kalkaska   MI
1951 - Unkwn
Type: 2 Frequency: 2
EEX, EXR, EXW

Great Lakes Fisherman
Westerville   OH
1973 -
Type: 4 Frequency: 2
UAP, GZD

Great Lakes Gazette
Grand Marais   MI
1973 - 1977
Type: 2 Frequency: 3
Earlier Title: People and Places
WIH

Great Lakes Sailor
Akron   OH
1987 -
Type: 4 Frequency: 2
DUD, CLE

Great Lakes Sportsman
Southfield   MI
1970 - Unkwn
Type: 4 Frequency: 3
EEX, MPI, VAP

Great Lakes Travel & Living
Port Clinton   OH
1986 -
Type: 2 Frequency: 2

Greater Indianapolis
Indianapolis   IN
1964 - 1970
Type: 1 Frequency: 2
ISL, XCA

Greater Lubbock Magazine
Lubbock   TX
1929 - Unkwn
Type: 1 Frequency: 5
IEA, IFA, ILU, IYU

Greater Philadelphia Magazine
Philadelphia   PA
1908 - 1967
Type: 1 Frequency: 2
DXU, PAU, TEU

Greater Portland Magazine
Portland   ME
1956 -
Type: 1 Frequency: 4
PPN, NYP

Greatlakes
Chicago   IL
1972 - Unkwn
Type: 4 Frequency: 4

Greenville Magazine
Greenville   SC
1981 -
Type: 1 Frequency: 2
SEA, SFU

Greenville Woman
Greenville   SC
1987 -
Type: 3 Frequency: 5
SGB, SWW

Gulf Coast Fisherman
Port Lavaca   TX
1977 -
Type: 4 Frequency: 4
Earlier Title: Harold Wells Gulf
Coast Fisherman

Gulf Coast Golfer
Houston   TX
1983 -
Type: 4 Frequency: 2

Gulfshore Life Magazine
Naples   FL
1970 -
Type: 2 Frequency: 2

H Magazine
Houston   TX
Unkwn - 1978
Type: 1 Frequency: Unkwn

Hampton Life
Southampton   NY
1974 - Unkwn
Type: 2 Frequency: 2

Hartford
Hatfield   MA
1982 - 1984
Type: 1 Frequency: 2

Hartford County Woman
Hartford   CT
Unkwn -
Type: 4 Frequency: 2

Hartford Monthly
Hartford   CT
Present
Type: 1 Frequency: 2
HPL, UCH

Hartford Woman
Stamford   CT
1981 -
Type: 3 Frequency: 2
HPL

Hawaii Profile
Honolulu   HI
1984 - Unkwn
Type: 2 Frequency: 2
HIL, HUH

Hawaii U S A
Honolulu   HI
1962 - Unkwn
Type: 2 Frequency: 1

Hawaiian Sportsman
Honolulu   HI
1948 - 1951
Type: Unkwn Frequency: 2
HHD

High Country
Council   ID
Unkwn - Unkwn
Type: 2 Frequency: 2

High Country
Bozeman   MT
1972 - 1973
Type: 2 Frequency: 5
MTL

High Country Living Magazine
Helen   GA
1978 - 1983
Type: 2 Frequency: 2
GUA

High Country Magazine
Placerville   CA
1982 -
Type: 2 Frequency: 2

High Country, The
Temecula   CA
1967 -
Type: 4 Frequency: 4
AZU, CDS, CUS, NYP

*Highlands of the Virginias Maga-
zine*
Covington   VA
1987 -
Type: 2 Frequency: 5

Hingham Town Crier
Hingham   MA
Unkwn - Unkwn
Type: 1 Frequency: Unkwn

Historic Bucks County
Doylestown   PA
1952 - Unkwn
Type: 2 Frequency: 4

Honolulu
Honolulu   HI
1966 -
Type: 1 Frequency: 2
Earlier Title: Paradise of the
Pacific
LPU

Hoosier Outdoors
Chestertown   IN
1968 -
Type: 4 Frequency: 3
IBS, IIB, IUE

Hoosierland Magazine
Indianapolis   IN
1962 - Unkwn
Type: 2 Frequency: 2

House in the Hamptons
Remsemberg   NY
1981 - Unkwn
Type: 4 Frequency: 5
SEU, SHI

Houston City Magazine
Houston   TX
1977 - 1987
Type: 1 Frequency: 2
DLC, IGA, IXA, TXH

Houston Goodlife
Houston   TX
1983 - Unkwn
Type: 1 Frequency: 2

Houston Home & Garden
Houston   TX
1974 -
Type: 3 Frequency: 5
DLC, IXA, TXA, TXG, TXN

Houston Living
Houston   TX
1973 -
Type: 1 Frequency: 3

Houston Metropolitan Magazine
Houston   TX
1974 -
Type: 1 Frequency: 3
DLC, IXA, TXA, TXH

Houston Monthly
Houston   TX
1971 -
Type: 1 Frequency: 2
HYP, TXN

Houston Northwest Magazine
Woodlands   TX
1976 -
Type: 1 Frequency: 3

Houston Scene Magazine
Houston   TX
1972 - Unkwn
Type: 1 Frequency: 2

Houston Town & Country Magazine
Houston   TX
1944 - Unkwn
Type: 1 Frequency: 2
TXH, TXN

Houston Woman
Houston   TX
Unkwn -
Type: Unkwn Frequency: 2

Houstonian Magazine
Houston   TX
1984 - 1986
Type: 1 Frequency: 2
Earlier Title: Houston Style
TXN

*Huckleberry: Magazine for the
New River Valley*
Christiansburg VA
1983 - 1984
Type: 2 Frequency: 5

Hudson Valley Living
Dobbs Ferry   NY
1983 - Unkwn
Type: 2 Frequency: 3

Hudson Valley Magazine
Woodstock   NY
1972 -
Type: 2 Frequency: 2
NYB, NYG, NYP

Humboldt County Magazine
Eureka   CA
1979 - Unkwn
Type: 2 Frequency: 4

Hyde Parker Magazine
Chicago   IL
1973 - Unkwn
Type: 1 Frequency: 3

Idaho Wildlife Review
Boise   ID
1948 - 1976
Type: 4 Frequency: 4
GUA, AUM, TKN, WYU

Idaho Yesterdays
Boise   ID
1957 -
Type: 4 Frequency: 4
DLC, GUA, MNU, NYP

Illinois Issues
Springfield   IL
1975 - Unkwn
Type: 4 Frequency: 2
CZL, IAC I, AF IA, L

*Illinois Magazine, The Magazine of
the Prairie State*
Litchfield   IL
1962 -
Type: 2 Frequency: 3
DLC, IAO, MUU

Images of Hampton Roads
Virginia Beach VA
1987 - Unkwn
Type: 2 Frequency: 2

In Kentucky
Frankfort   KY
1937 - Unkwn
Type: 2 Frequency: 3
Earlier Title: Kentucky Progress
Magazine
LPU, FUG, KEU, VA@

In New York Magazine
New York   NY
Unkwn - Unkwn
Type: 1 Frequency: 2

Indian River Life
Vero Beach   FL
1972 - Unkwn
Type: 2 Frequency: 5

Indian River Lifestyle
Ft Lauderdale FL
1982 - Unkwn
Type: 2 Frequency: 2

Indianapolis at Home
Indianapolis   IN
1977 - Unkwn
Type: 3 Frequency: 2
Earlier Title: Indianapolis Home &
Garden
IPL, ISL

Indianapolis Downtowner
Indianapolis   IN
1966 - 1972
Type: 1 Frequency: 2
ISL

Indianapolis Magazine
Indianapolis   IN
1962 -
Type: 1 Frequency: 2
Earlier Title: Greater Indianapolis
ISL, XCA

Indianapolis Monthly
Indianapolis   IN
1977 -
Type: 1 Frequency: 2
IPU, ISL

Indianapolis Woman
Indianapolis   IN
1984 -
Type: 3 Frequency: 2
IIB, ISL, XCA

Inland Empire
Riverside   CA
1976 -
Type: 2 Frequency: 2

Inland Shores
Elm Grove   WI
1977 - Unkwn
Type: 2 Frequency: 4
DLC, NRC, NYP, WIH

*Inland; The Magazine of the Mid-
dle West*
Chicago   IL
1953 -
Type: 2 Frequency: 4
JFK, SPI, MNU, MUU

Inside Chicago
Chicago   IL
1987 -
Type: 1 Frequency: 3
IBF, IBZ

Iowan, The
Shenandoah   IA
1952 -
Type: 2 Frequency: 4
IOU, IOV, IWA, UBY, VIC

Island Life
Sanibel   FL
1982 -
Type: 2 Frequency: 5

Island Monthly Reader, The
Siasconset   MA
Unkwn - Unkwn
Type: 2 Frequency: 5

Isle Camera, The
Grosse Ile   MI
1945 - Unkwn
Type: Unkwn Frequency: 3

INFO
New Haven   CT
1952 - Unkwn
Type: 1 Frequency: 2

Jackson Magazine
Jackson   MS
1977 -
Type: 1 Frequency: 2
Earlier Title: Jackson, The
Mississippi Magazine
EMU, MFM, MUM, NYP

Jacksonville Magazine
Jacksonville   FL
1963 -
Type: 1 Frequency: 5
FDA, FHM, FUG

Jacksonville Today
Jacksonville   FL
1985 -
Type: 1 Frequency: 2
FJD

K S Magazine
Wichita   KS
1978 -
Type: 1 Frequency: 2
Earlier Title: Wichitan
DLC, KKN, KSW

Kalamazoo
New York   NY
1958 - Unkwn
Type: 1 Frequency: 2

Kalamazoo Magazine
Kalamazoo   MI
1963 - 1966
Type: 1 Frequency: 2
DLC, EEX, EXW, NYP

Kansas City Homes & Gardens
Prairie View   KS
1986 -
Type: 4 Frequency: 3

Kansas City Magazine
Kansas City   MO
1976 -
Type: 1 Frequency: 2
SVP

Kansas City Town Squire
Prairie Village MO
1968 -
Type: 1 Frequency: 2

Kansas City Woman
Shawnee Missio   KS
Unkwn -
Type: 3 Frequency: 2

Kansas Game and Fish
Marietta   GA
Unkwn -
Type: 4 Frequency: Unkwn

Kansas!
Topeka   KS
1945 -
Type: 2 Frequency: 4
GUA, KFP, KSW

Kentucky Dossier
Louisville   KY
1983 -
Type: 2 Frequency: 4
KUK

Kentucky Golfer
Louisville   KY
1964 - Unkwn
Type: 4 Frequency: Unkwn

Kentucky Happy Hunting Ground
Frankfort   KY
1945 -
Type: 4 Frequency: 3
DLC, KUK

*Key Magazine/This Week in
Pittsburgh*
Pittsburgh   PA
1931 -
Type: 1 Frequency: 1

Knoxville Lifestyle
Knoxville   TN
1980 - 1983
Type: 1 Frequency: 3
TKN

L A Style
Los Angeles   CA
1985 -
Type: 1 Frequency: 2

L A West
Santa Monica   CA
1978 -
Type: 1 Frequency: 2
Earlier Title: Previous (Santa
Monica)

L A Woman
Los Angeles   CA
1985 -
Type: 3 Frequency: 3

La Jolla
La Jolla   CA
1984 -
Type: 2 Frequency: Unkwn

Lake Country
Roanoke   VA
1987 -
Type: 2 Frequency: 3

Lake Superior Magazine
Duluth   MN
1979 -
Type: 2 Frequency: 3
Earlier Title: Lake Superior Port
Cities

Lakeland Boating
Highland Park   IL
1946 -
Type: 4 Frequency: 2
BGU

Lancaster Magazine
Lancaster   PA
1950 - Unkwn
Type: 1 Frequency: 2

Lansing Magazine
Lansing   MI
Unkwn - Unkwn
Type: 1 Frequency: 2

Las Vegan
Las Vegas   NV
1976 -
Type: 1 Frequency: 2

Life & Home
Tarpon Springs FL
1982 -
Type: 2 Frequency: 3

Linking the Dots
Islesboro   ME
Unkwn -
Type: 2 Frequency: 3

Living in South Carolina
Columbia   SC
1950 -
Type: 2 Frequency: 2

Long Island Forum
Syosset   NY
1938 -
Type: 4 Frequency: 2

Long Island Home
Bethpage   NY
1951 - Unkwn
Type: 4 Frequency: 5

Long Island Life
Manhasset   NY
1982 - 1984
Type: 2 Frequency: 2
NYP, VVX, ZIH

Long Island Monthly
Long Island   NY
1988
Type: 2 Frequency: 2
SFO, VVX, XSU

Long Island Sportsman
Huntington   NY
1974 - Unkwn
Type: 4 Frequency: 2
ZQP

Long Island's Night Life
Deer Park   NY
1981 - Unkwn
Type: 4 Frequency: 5
Earlier Title: New York's Nightlife

Los Angeles FM & Fine Arts
New York   NY
1958 - Unkwn
Type: Unkwn Frequency: 2

Los Angeles Home and Garden
Canoga Park   CA
1980 - Unkwn
Type: 3 Frequency: 5

Los Angeles; the Magazine of
Southern California
Los Angeles   CA
1960 -
Type: 2 Frequency: 2
CSL, HDC, UIU

Louisiana Conservationist
New Orleans   LA
1948 -
Type: 4 Frequency: 3
Earlier Title: AAA FUG   GUA
LUU

Louisiana Game & Fish
Marietta   GA
1981 -
Type: 4 Frequency: Unkwn

Louisiana Journal
Baton Rouge   LA
1987 -
Type: 2 Frequency: 5
CEN, LNU, LRT, LUS

Louisiana Life
Metairie   LA
1981 -
Type: 2 Frequency: 3
DLC, CEN, LNU, LRT

Louisiana Magazette
Many   LA
1959 - 1963
Type: 4 Frequency: 4
LUU, LWA

Louisiana Magazine
New Orleans   LA
Unkwn - Unkwn
Type: 2 Frequency: Unkwn

Louisiana Woods & Water
Monroe   LA
1971 - Unkwn
Type: 4 Frequency: 2

Louisiana: This Month
Baton Rouge   LA
Unkwn - Unkwn
Type: Unkwn Frequency: Unkwn

Louisville Magazine
Louisville   KY
1950 -
Type: 1 Frequency: 2
KTS, DLC, NYP

Lynchburg
Lynchburg   VA
1968 - Unkwn
Type: 1 Frequency: 3
VCQ, VIC, VPI, VWM

Lynchburg All-American
Lynchburg   VA
1988
Type: 1 Frequency: 3

LI Magazine
Garden City   NJ
1972 - Unkwn
Type: 2 Frequency: 1

Macon Magazine
Macon   GA
1986 -
Type: 1 Frequency: 4

Madison Magazine
Madison   WI
1978 -
Type: 1 Frequency: 2
Earlier Title: Madison Select

Madison Select
Madison   WI
1965 - 1978
Type: 1 Frequency: 2
WIH

Magazine of Cambridge
Cambridge   MA
Unkwn - Unkwn
Type: 1 Frequency: Unkwn

Magazine of Utah, The
Salt Lake City UT
1984 - Unkwn
Type: 2 Frequency: 3

Maine
Machias   ME
Unkwn -
Type: 2 Frequency: 2

Maine Antique Digest
Waldoboro   ME
1973 -
Type: 4 Frequency: 2
SMI, BBH, MEA

Maine Digest
Rockport   ME
1966 - 1970
Type: Unkwn Frequency: 4
UMF, VTU

Maine Life Magazine
Auburn   ME
1946 -
Type: 2 Frequency: 3
DLC, BYN, MEA

Malibu
Malibu   CA
1984 - Unkwn
Type: 1 Frequency: 5

Manhattan Magazine
New York   NY
1983 -
Type: 1 Frequency: 4
Earlier Title: Studio 54

Manhattan, inc
New York   NY
1984 -
Type: 1 Frequency: 2
DLC, HUL, NYP

Marblehead Magazine; A Seacoast Journal
Marblehead   MA
1979 -
Type: 2 Frequency: 5

Maryland Conservationist
Annapolis   MD
1924 - Unkwn
Type: 4 Frequency: 3
DLC, MFS

Maryland Magazine
Annapolis   MD
1968 -
Type: 2 Frequency: 4
Earlier Title: Maryland
DLC, BAL, JHE, NYP

Mauian Magazine
Lahaina   HI
1984 -
Type: 2 Frequency: 2
HUH

Memphis
Memphis   TN
1976 -
Type: 1 Frequency: 2
TMA, TNS

Mesa Magazine
Mesa   AZ
1977 - Unkwn
Type: 1 Frequency: 2
AZU, MSA

Metro
Orange   CA
1986 -
Type: 4 Frequency: 3

Metro, The Magazine of South-eastern Virginia
Norfolk   VA
1970 - 1981
Type: 2 Frequency: 2
Earlier Title: Metro Hampton Roads Magazine

Metropolis; The Architecture and Design Magazine of New York
New York   NY
1982 -
Type: 3 Frequency: 2

Metropolitan Beaumont
Beaumont   TX
1976 - Unkwn
Type: 1 Frequency: 3
IXA, TXR

Metropolitan Detroit
Detroit   MI
1984 -
Type: 1 Frequency: 2
EEX, EYD, EYW

Metropolitan: Toledo and the
Northcoast
Toledo   OH
1987 -
Type: 2 Frequency: 3
BGU

Miami Mensual
Coral Gables   FL
1980 -
Type: 3 Frequency: 2
DLC, FQG, NYP

Miami Skier
Miami   FL
1986 - Unkwn
Type: 3 Frequency: Unkwn

Miami/South Florida Magazine
Miami   FL
1921 -
Type: 2 Frequency: 2
Earlier Title: Miami, the Magazine
of South Florida
FXG

Miamian, The
Miami   FL
1920 - 1972
Type: 1 Frequency: 5
Earlier Title: Miami Pictorial
DZM, FXG

Michigan Conservation
Lansing   MI
1931 - 1968
Type: 4 Frequency: 3
WDA

Michigan Environs
Grand Rapids   MI
1980 - 1982
Type: 1 Frequency: 3
EXC

Michigan Golfer
Brighton   MI
1982 -
Type: 4 Frequency: 3
EEX

Michigan Historical Review
Mt Pleasant   MI
1974 -
Type: 4 Frequency: 5
AAA, DLC, EEX, NYP, VA@

Michigan Living
Dearborn   MI
1918 -
Type: 2 Frequency: 2
DLC, UIU, EEX, EYP

Michigan Natural Resources Maga-
zine
Lansing   MI
1931 -
Type: 4 Frequency: 3
Earlier Title: Michigan
Conservaion
WDA

Michigan Out-of-Doors
Lansing   MI
1947 -
Type: 4 Frequency: 2

Michigan Woman
Farmington Hil MI
1984 -
Type: 4 Frequency: 3
EEP, EEX, EXG

Mid-Atlantic Country Magazine
Alexandria   VA
1980 -
Type: 2 Frequency: 2
Earlier Title: Country Magazine
DLC, UMC, NDD, VPI

Midwest Living, A Celebration of
the Heartland
Des Moines   IA
1987 -
Type: 2 Frequency: 3
IOQ, IOU, JID, NYP

Midwest Mariner
Chicago   IL
Unkwn - Unkwn
Type: 4 Frequency: 2

Midwest Motorist, The
St Louis   MO
1915 -
Type: 4 Frequency: 3

Midwest Outdoors
Burr Ridge   IL
1967 -
Type: 4 Frequency: 2
IIB, GZF

Midwest World
Columbus   OH
1973 -
Type: 2 Frequency: 2

Milwaukee
Milwaukee   WI
1956 - 1983
Type: 1 Frequency: 2
GZD, GZN G, ZQ

Milwaukee Impressions
Milwaukee   MI
Unkwn - Unkwn
Type: 1 Frequency: Unkwn
NYP, WIH

Milwaukee Magazine
Milwaukee   MI
1979 -
Type: 1 Frequency: 2
ILM, GZF, WKG

Minnesota Monthly
St Paul   MN
1964 -
Type: 2 Frequency: 2
EZT, DUD, MNU

Minnesota Sportsman
Marietta   GA
1977 -
Type: 4 Frequency: 2
DUD, MNJ, SPP

Minnesotan
St Paul   MN
1973 - Unkwn
Type: 2 Frequency: 4

Mississippi Coast
Gulfport   MS
1988
Type: 2 Frequency: 4

Mississippi Game & Fish
Marietta   GA
1937 -
Type: 4 Frequency: 2
KUK, MUM, YUS

Mississippi Magazine
Jackson   MS
1982 -
Type: 2 Frequency: 3

Mississippi News and Views
Jackson   MS
1962 - 1972
Type: 2 Frequency: 2
DPL, MCD M, FM MU, M

Mississippi Sportsman
Marietta   GA
1981 - Unkwn
Type: 4 Frequency: 5
MFM, NYP

*Mississippi; A View of the
Magnolia State*
Jackson   MS
1982 -
Type: 2 Frequency: 3

Missouri Conservationist
Jefferson City MO
1938 -
Type: 4 Frequency: 2
AAA, DLC, MNW, MUU

Missouri Highways
Jefferson City MO
1968 - 1973
Type: 2 Frequency: 3
KCP, MUU

Missouri Life
Chesterfield   MO
1973 -
Type: 2 Frequency: 4
DLC, KCP, MUU

Missouri; The Harbinger Magazine
Jefferson City MO
1968 - Unkwn
Type: 2 Frequency: 2

Mobile Bay Monthly
Mobile   AL
1985 -
Type: 2 Frequency: 2
AAA, ALM

Monroe
Monroe   MI
Present
Type: 2 Frequency: 3

Montana Magazine
Helena   MT
1970 -
Type: 2 Frequency: 3

Montana Outdoors
Helena   MT
1950 - 1970
Type: 4 Frequency: 5
AZU, YAM, MNP

Montana West: Magazine of the Northern Rockies
Helena   MT
1970 - Unkwn
Type: 2 Frequency: 4
WEA

Montana Wildlife
Helena   MT
1950 - 1970
Type: 4 Frequency: 5
AZU, ALM, YAM, WAU

Montana; the Magazine of Western History
Helena   MT
1951 -
Type: 4 Frequency: 4
DGW

Monterey Life
Monterey   CA
1979 -
Type: 2 Frequency: 2

Monthly Detroit
Detroit   MI
1978 -
Type: 1 Frequency: 2
DLC, EEM, EEX, NYP

Mountain Life and Work; Magazine of the Appalachian South
Clintwood   VA
1925 -
Type: 2 Frequency: 4
Earlier Title: Southern Mountain Life and Work
AAA, DGW, GUA, VA@, VPI

Mountain Living
Franklin   NC
1970 - 1983
Type: 2 Frequency: 2
NCS, NJB, TKN

Mountain Magazine
Conifer   CO
1983 - Unkwn
Type: 2 Frequency: 4

Mountainwest Magazine
Provo   UT
1975 - Unkwn
Type: 2 Frequency: 2

Museums New York
New York   NY
1980 - Unkwn
Type: 3 Frequency: 5
SMI, UIU

Myrtle Beach Magazine
Myrtle Beach   SC
1985 -
Type: 1 Frequency: 4
SUC

MPLS--St Paul Magazine
Minneapolis   MN
1972 -
Type: 1 Frequency: 2
DLC, MHS, MND

Naples Now
Naples   FL
1976 -
Type: 1 Frequency: 5
FUG

Nashville Magazine
Nashville   TN
1963 - 1970
Type: 1 Frequency: 2
TJC

Nashville!
Nashville   TN
1973 -
Type: 1 Frequency: 2
FUG, UMI, TJC, TKN

Nebraskaland
Lincoln   NB
1922 -
Type: 4 Frequency: 2
Earlier Title: Outdoor
Nebraskaland
DPL, SMI, AUM, LDL

Nevada Magazine
Carson City   NV
1936 -
Type: 2 Frequency: 3
IXA

New Bedford Magazine
Westbrook   MA
1981 -
Type: 2 Frequency: 3
BDR, SMU

New Black South
Sarasota   FL
1979 - Unkwn
Type: 4 Frequency: Unkwn

New Brooklyn
Brooklyn   NY
1978 -
Type: 1 Frequency: 4
Earlier Title: Staten Island Magazine
VDB

New Californian
Los Angeles   CA
Unkwn - Unkwn
Type: 2 Frequency: 2
CPP, MNU

New Charlotte Magazine
Charlotte   NC
1986 - Unkwn
Type: 1 Frequency: 2
DLC, NDD, NKM

New Chicago
Chicago   IL
Unkwn -
Type: 1 Frequency: 4

New Dominion
Alexandria   VA
1987 -
Type: 2 Frequency: 4
VAX, VPW

New East; Magazine of Eastern North Carolina
Edenton   NC
1973 - Unkwn
Type: 2 Frequency: 3

New England Bride
Sudbury   MA
1972 -
Type: 4 Frequency: 2
JCL

New England Galaxy
Sturbridge   MA
1959 - Unkwn
Type: 2 Frequency: 4

New England Getaways
Peabody   MA
1986 -
Type: 2 Frequency: 2
WZW

New England Living
Boston   MA
1949 - Unkwn
Type: 2 Frequency: Unkwn
DLC

New England Living
Worcester   MA
1984 -
Type: 2 Frequency: 3
GSU, WPF

New England Messenger
Lynn   MA
1972 - Unkwn
Type: 2 Frequency: Unkwn

New England Monthly
Haydenville   MA
1984 -
Type: 2 Frequency: 2
BPT, CTD, DLC

New England Racquet Sport
Edison   NJ
1979 -
Type: 4 Frequency: 3

New England Running
Brattleboro   VT
1978 -
Type: 4 Frequency: 2
FRQ

New England Sampler
Belfast   ME
1980 -
Type: 2 Frequency: 4
CTW, NYP

New England Senior Citizen
Weston   MA
1970 -
Type: 4 Frequency: 2

New England Sports
Boston   MA
Unkwn -
Type: 4 Frequency: 2

New England Sportsman
Frmingtn Hills MI
Unkwn - Unkwn
Type: 4 Frequency: 3

New Florida
Tequesta   FL
1981 - 1981
Type: 2 Frequency: 2
DLC, FDA, FUG

New Hampshire Echoes
Concord   NH
1970 - 1975
Type: 2 Frequency: 3
NYG

New Hampshire Profiles
Portsmouth   NH
1951 -
Type: 2 Frequency: 2
WIH

New Hampshire Spirit
Tamworth   NH
Present - Unkwn
Type: 2 Frequency: 4
NHM, NHS

New Haven
New Haven   CT
1982 - 1984
Type: 1 Frequency: 2

New Haven County Woman
Hamden   CT
1984 -
Type: 4 Frequency: 2

New Haven INFO Magazine
New Haven   CT
1952 - Unkwn
Type: 1 Frequency: 2
NHP, YUS

New Jersey Home & Garden
Monganville   NJ
1986 -
Type: 4 Frequency: 3
NJR

New Jersey Life
Maplewood   NJ
1931 - 1974
Type: 2 Frequency: 5
Earlier Title: Suburban Life and
Suburban New Jersey Life
NJL

New Jersey Living
Old Bridge   NJ
Unkwn - Unkwn
Type: 2 Frequency: 2
Earlier Title: Central New Jersey
Monthly
NJL, NJR

New Jersey Monthly
Morristown   NJ
1976 -
Type: 2 Frequency: 2
DLC, NJL, NJR, NYP

New Jersey Outdoors
Princeton   NJ
1950 -
Type: 4 Frequency: 2
DLC, NJL N, JR

New Jersey Shore Magazine
Egg Harbor Cit NJ
1980 - Unkwn
Type: 2 Frequency: 5

New Magazine
Piermont   NY
1964 -
Type: 2 Frequency: 5

New Mexico Magazine
Santa Fe   NM
1923 -
Type: 2 Frequency: 2
IRU, NMS, SUC, TXU

New Mexico Wildlife
Santa Fe   NM
1956 - Unkwn
Type: 4 Frequency: 3
IRU

New Norfolk Magazine
Norfolk   VA
1954 - 1978
Type: 1 Frequency: 2

New Orleanian
New Orleans   LA
1959 - Unkwn
Type: 1 Frequency: 2
LNU, LRU

New Orleans Magazine
New Orleans   LA
1966 -
Type: 1 Frequency: 2
DLC, LNU, LRU, VOD

New South
Atlanta   GA
1946 - 1973
Type: 2 Frequency: 4
DDU, FDA, NNM

New South Magazine, The
Lafayette   LA
1982 - Unkwn
Type: 2 Frequency: 3
DLC, GUA, NYP

New Texas
Austin   TX
1978 -
Type: 2 Frequency: 2
TXG

New Vistas
Miami   FL
Unkwn -
Type: 2 Frequency: 5
MPI

New Worlds
Irvine   CA
1970 - Unkwn
Type: 2 Frequency: 3

New York Alive
Albany   NY
1981 -
Type: 2 Frequency: 3
DLC, NYP

New York Family
New York   NY
1986 -
Type: 1 Frequency: 3

New York Habitat, For Co-op, Condominium and Loft Living
New York   NY
1982 -
Type: 3 Frequency: 5
NYP

New York Image
New York   NY
1984 -
Type: 1 Frequency: 5
NYP

New York Lifestyles
New York   NY
1987 -
Type: 1 Frequency: 3

New York Magazine
New York   NY
1968 -
Type: 1 Frequency: 1

New York Running News
New York   NY
1958 -
Type: 3 Frequency: 3

New York Sports
Brooklyn   NY
1983 - 1985
Type: 3 Frequency: 2

New York Woman
New York   NY
1986 -
Type: 3 Frequency: 3
DLC, HUL, RVE

New York's Nightlife
Deer Park   NY
1979 -
Type: 3 Frequency: 2

New Yorker, The
New York   NY
1923 -
Type: 2 Frequency: 1
DLC, IXA, NYP

Newark
Newark   NJ
Unkwn - Unkwn
Type: 1 Frequency: Unkwn

Newmonth: The Good Life in Up-
per Wisconsin
Denmark   WI
1975 -
Type: 2 Frequency: 2

Newport Beach
Beverly Hills   CA
1984 -
Type: 1 Frequency: 2

Nightbeat Magazine
Houston   TX
Unkwn -
Type: 3 Frequency: 2

Nor'westing
Edmonds   WA
1966 -
Type: 4 Frequency: 2

North Dakota Outdoors
Bismark   ND
1938 -
Type: 4 Frequency: 2
DLC, GUA, UND, NYP

North Dakota REC Magazine
Mandam   ND
1954 -
Type: 2 Frequency: 2

North Florida Living
Gainesville   FL
1984 - 1986
Type: 2 Frequency: 2
FDA, FUG

North Georgia Journal
Woodstock   GA
1984 -
Type: 4 Frequency: 4

North Shore Life Magazine
Glouchester   MA
1981 -
Type: 2 Frequency: 4

North Shore; the Magazine of
Chicago's Northern Suburbs
Winnetka   IL
1978 -
Type: 1 Frequency: 2
IHV

North Shore, the Magazine for
Living on the Gold Coast
Mineola   NY
1977 - Unkwn
Type: 2 Frequency: 3
NBT

North Texas Golfer
Houston   TX
1986 -
Type: 4 Frequency: 5

Northcoast View
Eureka   CA
1982 -
Type: 2 Frequency: 2
CHU

Northeast Magazine
Avoca   PA
Unkwn -
Type: 2 Frequency: 3
Earlier Title: Magazine of
Pennsylvania's Northeast

Northeast Outdoors
Waterbury   CT
1968 -
Type: 4 Frequency: 2

Northern Adventures Magazine; a
Magazine on Alaska
Wasilli ·   AK
1986 -
Type: 2 Frequency: 3

Northern Arizona Scenes
Manassas   VA
1976 -
Type: 2 Frequency: 5

Northern California Home & Gar-
den
City: Unkwn   CA
1987 - Unkwn
Type: 4 Frequency: 2

Northern Ohio Live
Cleveland   OH
1980 -
Type: 2 Frequency: 2
CLE, CSU, OBE

Northern Virginian
Vienna   VA
1971 -
Type: 2 Frequency: 3
Earlier Title: Virginia Cardinal
TNS, VAX, VGM, VIC

Northfield Magazine, The
Northfield   MN
1987 -
Type: 1 Frequency: 4
MHS, MNO

Northshore Magazine
Mandeville   LA
1984 - Unkwn
Type: 2 Frequency: 2
LRU, LSM

Northwest America
Boise   ID
1975 - Unkwn
Type: 2 Frequency: 3
DWC, IOQ, COO

Northwest Experience
Moscow   ID
1972 - Unkwn
Type: 2 Frequency: 4

Northwest Golfer
Bellevue   WA
1973 -
Type: 4 Frequency: 3

Northwest Living
Edmonds   WA
1983 -
Type: 2 Frequency: 2
Earlier Title: Northwest Edition
DLC, ORE, OSE, WAU

Northwest Ruralite
Portland   OR
1954 - 1973
Type: 2 Frequency: 2
ORU, OSO

Now in Stark County
Canton   OH
1978 - Unkwn
Type: 2 Frequency: 2

O Magazine
Omaha   NE
1984 -
Type: 1 Frequency: 2

*Ocooch Mountain News; A Maga-
zine of Southwest Wisconsin*
Gillingham   WI
1974 - 1981
Type: 2 Frequency: 2
GZU, WIH

Of Westchester Magazine
Mamaroneck   NY
1969 - Unkwn
Type: 2 Frequency: Unkwn
NYC, NYD

Off P'Tree
Atlanta   GA
1977 - Unkwn
Type: 1 Frequency: 2
GSU

*Offshore, New England's Boating
Magazine*
Needham   MA
1976 -
Type: 4 Frequency: 2
Earlier Title: New England Off-
shore

Oh! Idaho
Hailey   ID
Present
Type: 2 Frequency: 4

Ohio Fisherman
Westerville   OH
1966 -
Type: 4 Frequency: 2
OGC

Ohio Magazine
Columbus   OH
1977 -
Type: 2 Frequency: 2
DLC, LNC, OCP, OUN

Ohio River Magazine
Cincinnati   OH
Unkwn - Unkwn
Type: 4 Frequency: 5

Okc
Midwest City   OK
Unkwn - Unkwn
Type: Unkwn Frequency: 2

Oklahoma City Metro
Tulsa   OK
1982 - Unkwn
Type: 1 Frequency: 3

Oklahoma Game & Fish
Marietta   GA
1983 -
Type: 4 Frequency: 2

Oklahoma Home & Lifestyle
Tulsa   OK
1982 -
Type: 2 Frequency: 3
Earlier Title: Oklahoma Home &
Garden
OKS, OKT

Oklahoma Living Magazine
Oklahoma City   OK
Unkwn - Unkwn
Type: 2 Frequency: 3

Oklahoma Today
Oklahoma City   OK
1956 -
Type: 2 Frequency: 3
NYG, OKN, OKU, TXA

Old Florida Cracker
Tallahassee   FL
1956 - Unkwn
Type: 2 Frequency: 2
NYP

Old West
Austin   TX
1964 -
Type: 4 Frequency: 4
DLC, IRU, TXA, TXN

Omaha Magazine
Omaha   NE
1976 -
Type: 1 Frequency: 2
BCN

Omaha Profile
Omaha   NE
Unkwn - Unkwn
Type: 1 Frequency: Unkwn

Omnibus and Chicago FM Guide
Kenilworth   IL
1963 - Unkwn
Type: Unkwn Frequency: 2

On the Sound
Eastchester   NY
1971 -
Type: 2 Frequency: 2
CTL, UBM, SFO

On The Shore
Byram   CT
1972 - 1972
Type: 2 Frequency: 2
NJL

*Orange Coast Magazine, The Mag-
azine of Orange County*
Costa Mesa   CA
1974 -
Type: 2 Frequency: 2
CLB, CUI

Orange County Gentry
Costa Mesa   CA
1983 -
Type: 2 Frequency: 5

Orange County Home & Garden
Laguna Beach   CA
1979 - 1982
Type: 4 Frequency: 2
CUI

Orange County Illustrated
Newport Beach   CA
1962 - 1981
Type: 2 Frequency: 2
CFI, CLB, NYP

Orange County Magazine
Irvine   CA
1979 -
Type: 2 Frequency: 3

Orange County Magazine
Santa Ana   CA
1957 - 1967
Type: 2 Frequency: 2
CFI, LPU

Oregon Coast
Florence   OR
1982 -
Type: 2 Frequency: 3
SOI, LNU, OHY, ORE, WAU

Oregon Magazine
Portland   OR
1971 -
Type: 2 Frequency: 2
WIH

Oregon Outdoors
Hillsboro   OR
1967 -
Type: 4 Frequency: 5
OSO

Oregon Times Magazine
Portland   OR
1971 - 1977
Type: 2 Frequency: 2
OHY, ORE, ORU

Orlando Magazine
Orlando   FL
1946 - 1981
Type: 1 Frequency: 5
FTU, FUG, NYP

Orlando Monthly
Orlando   FL
1983 - Unkwn
Type: 1 Frequency: 5

Orlando-Land Magazine
Orlando   FL
1946 - 1981
Type: 1 Frequency: 2
FUG

Outdoor Arizona
Phoenix   AZ
1964 - 1979
Type: 4 Frequency: 2
AZN, AZS A, ZU

Outdoor California
Sacramento   CA
1930 -
Type: 4 Frequency: 3
ALM, CUS, CUZ, DLC

Outdoor Indiana
Indianapolis   IN
1934 -
Type: 4 Frequency: 5
DLC, FUG, IND, IUP

Outdoor Oklahoma
Oklahoma City   OK
1945 -
Type: 4 Frequency: 3
NYG, OKC, OKU

Outdoors in Georgia
Atlanta   GA
1966 - 1978
Type: 4 Frequency: 2
Earlier Title: Georgia Game and
Fish
AAA, DLC, GSU, GUA

Ozarks Mountaineer
Branson   MO
1952 -
Type: 2 Frequency: 3
AFU, AKC, DLC

Pacific Life
Santa Cruz   CA
1981 - Unkwn
Type: 2 Frequency: 2

Pacific Magazine
Honolulu   HI
1976 -
Type: 2 Frequency: 5
CUS, CUZ, HUH

Pacific Northwest
Seattle   WA
1966 -
Type: 2 Frequency: 2
Earlier Title: Pacific Search
LPU, DLC, OHY, ORU

Pacific Scene
Fresno   CA
1960 - Unkwn
Type: 2 Frequency: 2
CPO, LPU

Pacific Skipper
Los Angeles   CA
1974 - Unkwn
Type: 4 Frequency: 2
DLC

Pacific Wilderness Journal
Portland   OR
1973 - Unkwn
Type: 2 Frequency: 3

Pacifica Magazine
Arcata   CA
1971 - Unkwn
Type: 2 Frequency: Unkwn

Palm Beach Illustrated
W Palm Beach   FL
Unkwn - Unkwn
Type: 1 Frequency: 2

Palm Beach Life
Palm Beach   FL
1906 -
Type: 1 Frequency: 2
FDA, FHM, NYP

Palm Beach Social Pictorial
Palm Beach   FL
1953 -
Type: 3 Frequency: 1

Palm Springs Life
Palm Springs   CA
1958 -
Type: 1 Frequency: 2
CLB, CNB, LPU

Palm Springs Villager
Palm Springs   CA
Unkwn - 1959
Type: 1 Frequency: 2
LLU, LPU

Panorama Magazine
Rockford   IL
1978 - Unkwn
Type: 2 Frequency: 2

Panorama, The Magazine of Bucks County
Doylestown   PA
1959 - Unkwn
Type: Unkwn Frequency: 2
LQS, PHA, PIT

Paradise of the Pacific Magazine
Honolulu   HI
1888 - 1965
Type: 2 Frequency: 2
CLU, HUH, VA@

Park Avenue Social Review
New York   NY
1925 -
Type: 1 Frequency: 2

Park East
New York   NY
1964 - Unkwn
Type: 1 Frequency: 2
NYP

Park East: The Magazine of New York
New York   NY
1940 - 1954
Type: 1 Frequency: Unkwn
NYG

Parkway, The Magazine for New North Dallas
Dallas   TX
1982 - 1983
Type: 1 Frequency: 2
IGA, ISM

Pasadena Magazine
Pasadena   CA
1974 - Unkwn
Type: 1 Frequency: 2
CPP, LPU

Peachtree Magazine
Atlanta   GA
Unkwn -
Type: 1 Frequency: 2

Peninsula
Redwood City   CA
1985 -
Type: 2 Frequency: 2

Peninsula Magazine
Palo Alto   CA
1975 - Unkwn
Type: 2 Frequency: 2

Peninsula Magazine
Sequin   WA
1986 - Unkwn
Type: 2 Frequency: 3
EOS, WAU

Pennsylvania Angler
Harrisburg   PA
1931 -
Type: 4 Frequency: 2
DLC, MUU, NRC, DXU, PVU

Pennsylvania Game News
Harrisburg   PA
1930 -
Type: 4 Frequency: 2
LKC, SRS, WAU

Pennsylvania Heritage
Harrisburg   PA
1967 -
Type: 4 Frequency: 4
NYP, DXU, PAU, PIT, VPI

Pennsylvania Illustrated
Camp Hill   PA
1976 - Unkwn
Type: 2 Frequency: 3
Earlier Title: Pittsburgher Magazine
DLC, PBU, PHA

Pennsylvania Magazine
Camp Hill   PA
1981 -
Type: 2 Frequency: 3
DLC, NYP, PBU, PSC

Pennsylvania Outdoors
Oshkosh   WI
1982 -
Type: 4 Frequency: 5
DLC, UPM

Pennsylvania Sportsman
Harrisburg   PA
1959 -
Type: 4 Frequency: 5
PHA, UPM

People of North Carolina
Raleigh   NC
1977 - 1978
Type: Unkwn Frequency: Unkwn

Philadelphia Magazine
Philadelphia   PA
1908 -
Type: 1 Frequency: 2
Earlier Title: Greater Philadelphia
EAS, LAS

Phoenix Home & Garden
Phoenix   AZ
1980 -
Type: 3 Frequency: 2
AZT, AZU, DLC, IGA

Phoenix Living
Dallas   TX
1979 - 1983
Type: 1 Frequency: 3
MSA

Phoenix Magazine
Phoenix   AZ
1966 -
Type: 1 Frequency: 2
AZT, AZS, AZU

Pictorial Life; The Society Journal of the Gold Coast
Ft Lauderdale FL
1965 - Unkwn
Type: 2 Frequency: 5

Pittsburgh Magazine
Pittsburgh   PA
1969 -
Type: 1 Frequency: 2
Earlier Title: Pittsburgh Renaissance
DLC, NYP, DUQ, PIT

Pittsburgher Magazine
Pittsburgh   PA
1977 - 1981
Type: 1 Frequency: 2
Earlier Title: Pennsylvania Illustrated
DLC, HYP, PIT

Plainswoman
Grand Fork   ND
1977 -
Type: 4 Frequency: 2
WIH

Plantation Monthly
Plantation   FL
1987 -
Type: 1 Frequency: 2

Playground of the Rockies
Denver   CO
1958 - Unkwn
Type: 2 Frequency: 3
DPL

Playsure Magazine
Houston   TX
1976 - 1980
Type: 2 Frequency: 2

Pleasant Hawaii
Honolulu   HI
1988
Type: 2 Frequency: 4

Point West
Phoenix   AZ
1959 - 1962
Type: 2 Frequency: 2
AZT, PNX, DPL

Politics New England
Dedham   MA
1981 - Unkwn
Type: 4 Frequency: 2
MAS, NHS

Portland
Portland   OR
1974 - 1987
Type: 1 Frequency: 2
DPL, OEL, OHY, OPU, ORU

Ports South
Beaufort   SC
1979 - 1980
Type: 2 Frequency: 2

Posh
Charlotte   NC
Unkwn - Unkwn
Type: 1 Frequency: 3

Potomac Appalachian
Washington   DC
1973 - Unkwn
Type: 4 Frequency: 2
DLC, ANC

Princeton Magazine
Princeton   NJ
1982 - Unkwn
Type: 1 Frequency: 2
NJL, PPR

Prosperous Times
Hammond   IN
1988
Type: 2 Frequency: 3

*Quality of Life in Loisaida; the
Lower East Side Magazine*
New York   NY
1977 -
Type: 1 Frequency: 3

Queen City
Cincinnati   OH
1980
Type: 1 Frequency: Unkwn

Raleigh
Raleigh   NC
1969 - 1972
Type: 1 Frequency: 3
NRC

*Ranch & Coast: The Magazine of
the California Riviera*
Solana Beach   CA
1964 -
Type: 2 Frequency: 2

*Rayburn's Ozark Guide; The
Magazine of the Ozarks*
Eureka Springs AR
1943 - Unkwn
Type: 2 Frequency: 4
AKU, AST, CLU, IUL

Rhode Island Monthly
Providence   RI
Present
Type: 2 Frequency: 2
RHI, RIU

Rhode Island Woman
Cranston   RI
1986 -
Type: 4 Frequency: 2

Richmond Lifestyle
Richmond   VA
1979 - 1982
Type: 1 Frequency: 2
NDD, NNM, VLW, VRU

Richmond Magazine
Richmond   VA
1974 - 1979
Type: 1 Frequency: 2
VIC, VLW, VRU

*Right Here, The Hometown Maga-
zine*
Huntington   IN
1984 -
Type: 1 Frequency: 3

River Cities; the Magazine of Shreveport and Bossier
Shreveport   LA
1981 -
Type: 1 Frequency: 2
AFU, CEN, LNU, LUU, MFM

Roanoker, The
Roanoke   VA
1974 -
Type: 1 Frequency: 2
NYP, VIC, VMI, VPI

Rockford Magazine
Rockford   IL
1986 -
Type: 1 Frequency: 2
SPI

Rockies Magazine, The
Provo   UT
1970 - Unkwn
Type: 2 Frequency: 3

Rocky Mountain Magazine
St James   CO
1979 - 1982
Type: 2 Frequency: 2
Earlier Title: Colorado/Rocky Mountain West
AZU, LPU, COS, DUP, DLC

Rural Arkansas Magazine
Little Rock   AR
1946 -
Type: 2 Frequency: 2
AFU

Rural Electric Nebraskan
Lincoln   NB
1947 -
Type: 2 Frequency: 2
Earlier Title: Nebraska Electric Farmer
AGL

Rural Georgia
Atlanta   GA
1945 -
Type: 2 Frequency: 2
GUA

Rural Kentuckian
Louisville   KY
1948 -
Type: 2 Frequency: 2
KBE, KCC, KEU

Rural Living
Richmond   VA
1946 -
Type: 2 Frequency: 2
VAX, VA@, VPI, VRU

Rural Missouri
Jefferson City MO
1948 -
Type: 2 Frequency: 2
Earlier Title: Rural Electric Missourian
AGL

Rural Montana
Great Falls   MT
1952 -
Type: 2 Frequency: 2
Earlier Title: Montana Rural Electric News

Rural Vermonter
East Thetford   VT
1962 - 1966
Type: 2 Frequency: 2
AQM, WIH

Ruralite
Forest Grove   OR
1954 -
Type: 2 Frequency: 2
Earlier Title: Northwest Ruralite
OHY, ORU, OSO

RSVP, The Magazine of Good Living
Honolulu   HI
1984 -
Type: 2 Frequency: 2
HUH

S. A.
San Antonio   TX
1978 - 1980
Type: 1 Frequency: 2
Earlier Title: San Antonio
IGA, TXJ

Sacramento Magazine
Sacramento   CA
1975 -
Type: 1 Frequency: 2
Earlier Title: Sacramento Valley Magazine

Salt Magazine
Kennebunkport   ME
1973 -
Type: 2 Frequency: 4
CTW, DLC, BBH, BYN

Sam Houston's Metropolitan Magazine
Houston   TX
Unkwn - 1978
Type: 1 Frequency: Unkwn

San Angelo Magazine
San Angelo   TX
1983 -
Type: 1 Frequency: 2
IXA, IYU

San Antonio Homes & Gardens
San Antonio   TX
1985 -
Type: 3 Frequency: 2

San Antonio Living
San Antonio   TX
1978 - 1983
Type: 1 Frequency: 3

San Antonio Monthly
San Antonio   TX
1981 -
Type: 1 Frequency: 2
SNM, TNY, TXJ

San Antonio Today
San Antonio   TX
1984 - Unkwn
Type: 1 Frequency: 2
IXA, TXJ

San Diego Home/Garden
San Diego   CA
1979 -
Type: 3 Frequency: 2
CDS, CUS, DLC, IQA

San Diego Magazine
San Diego   CA
1948 -
Type: 1 Frequency: 2
Earlier Title: San Diego & Point
Magazine
CLU

San Diego Woman
San Diego   CA
1983 -
Type: 3 Frequency: 2

San Fernando Valley
Sherman Oaks   CA
1957 - 1977
Type: 2 Frequency: 2
Earlier Title: San Fernando Valley
& Que Magazine
CNO, LPU

San Francisco Focus
San Francisco   CA
1953 -
Type: 1 Frequency: 2
CSF, CSJ, CUZ, DLC

San Francisco Goodlife
San Francisco   CA
1982 - Unkwn
Type: 1 Frequency: 5

San Francisco Magazine
San Francisco   CA
1957 - Unkwn
Type: 1 Frequency: 2
CLU, CUS, MPI, SDS

San Francisco: The Magazine
San Francisco   CA
1987 -
Type: 1 Frequency: 2
CLU, CUZ, FUG, HUL

San Gabriel Valley Magazine
Alhambra   CA
1976 - Unkwn
Type: 2 Frequency: 3
CLA, CSL

*Sandlapper; The Magazine of
South Carolina*
Columbia   SC
1968 - 1982
Type: 2 Frequency: 5

Santa Barbara
Santa Barbara   CA
1906
Type: 1 Frequency: 2
CLU, LPU

Santa Fean
Santa Fe   NM
1972 -
Type: 1 Frequency: 2
AZU, LPU, IQU, IRU

Sara Bay Monthly
City: Unkwn   FL
1983 - Unkwn
Type: 2 Frequency: 5

Sarasota
Sarasota   FL
1979 -
Type: 1 Frequency: 2
Earlier Title: Clubhouse Magazine

Sarasota Town & Country Magazine
Sarasota   FL
1976 -
Type: 1 Frequency: 5
Earlier Title: Sarasota Magazine
FUG

Saratoga - The Magazine
Saratoga Spring NY
1979 - Unkwn
Type: 1 Frequency: 2

Savannah Magazine
Savannah   GA
1969 - 1979
Type: 1 Frequency: 2
GUA

Scenic Idaho
Boise   ID
1946 - Unkwn
Type: 2 Frequency: 4
LPU, DPL, UUM, WEA

Scenic South
Louisville   KY
1944 - 1946
Type: 2 Frequency: 2
AAA, ALM, FUG, KEU, PIT

Scenic Southwest
Williams   AZ
1942 - 1957
Type: 2 Frequency: 2
AZS

Scottsdale Magazine
Scottsdale   AZ
1980 -
Type: 1 Frequency: 4
AZD, AZU

Scottsdale Scene Magazine
Scottsdale   AZ
1983
Type: 1 Frequency: 2
AZU

Seacoast Life
North Hampton   NH
1985 -
Type: 2 Frequency: 4
NHM

Seacoast Woman
Portsmouth   NH
1977 -
Type: 4 Frequency: 1
NHM

Seattle Magazine
Seattle   WA
1964 -
Type: 1 Frequency: 2

Seattle Woman, The Magazine with a New View
Seattle   WA
1983 - Unkwn
Type: 3 Frequency: 2
WAU, WIH

Sedona Life
Sedona   AZ
1976 - Unkwn
Type: 1 Frequency: 2

Senior, California Senior's Magazine
San Luis Obisp CA
1981 -
Type: 4 Frequency: 2

Shreveport
Shreveport   LA
1920 - 1987
Type: 1 Frequency: 2
Earlier Title: Shreveport Magazine
CEN, LNU, LRU, LUU

*Sierra Life Magazine, The Maga-
zine of the High Sierra*
Bishop   CA
1981 -
Type: 2 Frequency: 3
LPU

Single Life Milwaukee
Milwaukee   WI
1983 -
Type: 3 Frequency: 3
GZD

Sioux City Magazine
Sioux City   IA
1973 - Unkwn
Type: 1 Frequency: 2
IOQ

*Ski South, The Magazine of
Southern Skiers*
Roanoke   VA
Unkwn - Unkwn
Type: 4 Frequency: 5
NRC, VPI

Snowmobile West
Idaho Falls   ID
1974 -
Type: 4 Frequency: 3
AZH

South Bay Magazine
Redondo Beach   CA
1978 - Unkwn
Type: 2 Frequency: 3
CGE, LPU

South Carolina History Illustrated
Columbia   SC
Unkwn - Unkwn
Type: 4 Frequency: 4
DLC

South Carolina Magazine
Columbia   SC
1937 -
Type: 2 Frequency: 3
WIH

South Carolina Wildlife
Columbia   SC
1954 -
Type: 4 Frequency: 3
DLC, GUA, DSC, SEA, SUC

South Florida Home & Garden
Miami   FL
1984 -
Type: 4 Frequency: 5

South Florida Living
Deerfield Beach FL
1981 - Unkwn
Type: 2 Frequency: 3

South Florida Outdoors
Miami   FL
1980 - Unkwn
Type: 4 Frequency: 2

South Illustrated
Birmingham   AL
1964 - Unkwn
Type: 2 Frequency: 2

South Jersey
Millville   NJ
1979 -
Type: 2 Frequency: 2

South Magazine, The
Tampa   FL
1974 - 1980
Type: 2 Frequency: 2
ALM, FHM, GUA, NYP

South; the News Magazine of Dixie
Birmingham   AL
1936 - Unkwn
Type: 4 Frequency: 2
Earlier Title: Alabama; the News
Magazine of the Deep South
AAA, ABC, WIH

Southeast Ohio
Athens   OH
1969 -
Type: 2 Frequency: 5

Southeastern
New London   CT
1982 - Unkwn
Type: 2 Frequency: 3

Southern Accents
Birmingham   AL
1977 -
Type: 4 Frequency: 3
AAA, DLC, GUA, SUC

Southern Boating Magazine
Miami   FL
1972 -
Type: 4 Frequency: 2
DZM

Southern Bodybuilder
Knoxville   TN
1983 - Unkwn
Type: 4 Frequency: 2

Southern Bowler
Atlanta   GA
1957 - Unkwn
Type: 4 Frequency: Unkwn

Southern Bride
Greensboro   NC
Present
Type: 4 Frequency: 3

Southern California Living
Buena Park   CA
Unkwn -
Type: 4 Frequency: 3

Southern California Sports Guide
Encino   CA
1975 - Unkwn
Type: 4 Frequency: 3

Southern Exposure
Durham   NC
1973 -
Type: 4 Frequency: 3
FHS, SVP, NPC

Southern Gardening
Forsyth   GA
1949 - 1950
Type: 4 Frequency: 4
GUA

Southern Gardens
Columbia   SC
1960 - Unkwn
Type: 4 Frequency: 3

Southern Golf
Clearwater   FL
1969 -
Type: 4 Frequency: 3

Southern Golfer
Jackson   MS
1955 - Unkwn
Type: 4 Frequency: Unkwn
Earlier Title: The Mississippi
Golfer

Southern Homes
Atlanta   GA
1983 -
Type: 4 Frequency: 3
FHM, ERE

Southern Living
Birmingham   AL
1966 -
Type: 2 Frequency: 2
ALM, AFU, FDA, SUC

Southern Magazine
Little Rock   AR
1986 -
Type: 2 Frequency: 2
AAA, AAU, AFU, AKU, NYP

Southern Outdoors Magazine
Montgomery   AL
1953 -
Type: 4 Frequency: 5
Earlier Title: Southern
Outdoors/Gulf Coast Fisherman
GUA

Southern Partisan
Columbia   SC
1979 -
Type: 4 Frequency: 4
ALM, DLC, GUA, NYP, SEA

Southern Star
Ft. Lauderdale FL
1984 -
Type: 4 Frequency: 2

Southern Style
Knoxville   TN
1987 -
Type: 4 Frequency: 3

Southern Travel
New York   NY
1987 -
Type: 2 Frequency: 3
SGQ, SUC

Southern Vermont Magazine
Brattleboro   VT
1985 -
Type: 2 Frequency: 3
VTU

Southern Voices
Atlanta   GA
1974
Type: 2 Frequency: 3
Earlier Title: New South
AAA, ARU, FUG, GUA, AUM

Southern Waterways
Fort Myers   FL
1961 -
Type: 4 Frequency: 2
GPG

Southern World
Hilton Head Is SC
1979 - 1981
Type: 2 Frequency: 3
ALM, GUA, LUU, SEA, VIC

*Southlander; Magazine of the His-
toric South*
Birmingham   AL
1974
Type: 2 Frequency: 4
Earlier Title: Alabama News Re-
view
ALM

Southwest Art
Houston   TX
1971 -
Type: 4 Frequency: 2
Earlier Title: Southwest Art Gal-
lery Magazine
AZU, DPL, DLM, IGA

Southwest Magazine
Clovis   NM
1977 - Unkwn
Type: 2 Frequency: 3

Southwest Profile
Santa Fe   NM
1978 -
Type: 2 Frequency: 5

Southwest Skier
Studio City   CA
1966 - Unkwn
Type: 4 Frequency: 5
Earlier Title: Southern California
Skier

Southwest Woman
San Antonio   TX
1980 - 1982
Type: 4 Frequency: 2
IGA

Southwesterner
Columbus   NM
1961 - Unkwn
Type: 2 Frequency: 2
AZU, PNX, DPL

Spokane Magazine
Spokane   WA
1977 - Unkwn
Type: 1 Frequency: 2
WAU

Sports West
Provo   UT
1970 - Unkwn
Type: 4 Frequency: 2

Sportswise Philadelphia
New York   NY
1984 - Unkwn
Type: 3 Frequency: 3

Spotlight on Harrison
Rye   NY
1977 - Unkwn
Type: 1 Frequency: 2
VVW

Spotlight on Mamaroneck
Rye   NY
1977 - Unkwn
Type: 1 Frequency: 2
VVW

Spotlight on Rye
Rye   NY
1977 - Unkwn
Type: 1 Frequency: 2
VVW

Spotlighting Nebraska
Columbus   WA
1964 -
Type: 2 Frequency: 4
LDL

Springfield! Magazine
Springfield   MO
1979 -
Type: 1 Frequency: 2
SPI, SVP

Springfield/Hartford
Springfield   MA
1977 - Unkwn
Type: 1 Frequency: 2
Earlier Title: Springfield and Four
County News
MAS

St George Magazine
St George   UT
1984 - Unkwn
Type: 1 Frequency: 4
UUM

St Joseph Magazine
St Joseph   MO
1977 - Unkwn
Type: 1 Frequency: 2

St Louis Magazine
St Louis   MO
1963 -
Type: 1 Frequency: 2
Earlier Title: St Louisan
SOI

*State; Down Home in North
Carolina*
Raleigh   NC
1933 -
Type: 2 Frequency: 2
NDD, NDO, NCS

Stratton-Bromley Magazine
Stratton Mounta VT
1974 -
Type: 2 Frequency: 4
VTU

*Sunset; the Magazine of Western
Living*
Menlo Park   CA
1898 -
Type: 2 Frequency: 2
AAA, DDU, FDA, ORU, VA@

Surfing East
Ridgewood   NJ
1965 - Unkwn
Type: 4 Frequency: 3

Susquehanna Monthly Magazine
Marietta   PA
1976 -
Type: 2 Frequency: 2
Earlier Title: Susquehanna

Susquehanna Valley
Lewisburg   PA
1980 - Unkwn
Type: 2 Frequency: 2

Syracuse Magazine
Syracuse   NY
Unkwn - Unkwn
Type: 1 Frequency: 3
SYB

Tahoe Today
Zaphyr Cove   NV
1981 -
Type: 1 Frequency: 4

Tallahassee Magazine
Tallahassee   FL
1979 -
Type: 1 Frequency: 4
FDA

Tally
Wethersfield   CT
Unkwn - Unkwn
Type: Unkwn Frequency: Unkwn

Tampa Bay Life
Tampa   FL
Present
Type: 2 Frequency: 2

Tampa Bay Magazine
Tampa Bay   FL
1977 - 1983
Type: 1 Frequency: 5
Earlier Title: Tampa Magazine
FHM, FUG, NYP

Tampa Bay Metro Magazine
Tampa Bay   FL
1983 -
Type: 1 Frequency: 2
Earlier Title: Tampa Bay Monthly
FHM, FUG

Tampa Bay New Homes
Tampa   FL
1988
Type: 4 Frequency: 5

Tampa Bay--The Suncoast Magazine
Clearwater   FL
1986 -
Type: 1 Frequency: 3

Tampa/St Petersburg
Tampa   FL
1980 - Unkwn
Type: 1 Frequency: 2

Tar Heel; The Magazine of North Carolina
Greenville   NC
1977 - 1982
Type: 2 Frequency: 3
DLC, FUG, NCS, NGU, NRC

Tempo Magazine; Life in Northeastern Pennsylvania
Scranton   PA
1983 -
Type: 2 Frequency: 2
SCR, UPM

Tennessee Conservationist
Nashville   TN
1937 -
Type: 4 Frequency: 2
AAA, SOI, COO, TJC, TKN

Tennessee Illustrated
Knoxville   TN
Present
Type: 2 Frequency: 3
TKN, TNS

Tennessee Magazine
Nashville   TN
1958 -
Type: 2 Frequency: 2
AGL, TKN, TNS, TXM

Tennessee Sportsman
Marietta   GA
1980 -
Type: 4 Frequency: 2
TKN, TNS

Texas Fisherman
Houston   TX
1973 -
Type: 4 Frequency: 3
IXA, IYU T, XN

Texas Gardener
Waco   TX
1981 -
Type: 4 Frequency: 3
IXA, IYU, TXA

Texas Highways Magazine
Austin   TX
1953 -
Type: 2 Frequency: 2
DLC, SOI, NYG, IXA, IYU

Texas Hill Country Scenes
San Antonio   TX
1981 -
Type: 2 Frequency: Unkwn

Texas Homes
Dallas   TX
1977 - 1987
Type: 4 Frequency: 5
IGA, IXA, IYU, TXN

Texas Metro; Magazine of Texas Living
Fort Worth   TX
1965 -
Type: 2 Frequency: 2
Earlier Title: Texas Metro Magazine
ICU, IFA, IGA

Texas Monthly
Austin   TX
1973 -
Type: 2 Frequency: 2
DLC, DLM, NYP, ICU, IXA, TXN

Texas Parade
Austin   TX
1936 - 1978
Type: 2 Frequency: 2
IGA, IXA, IYU, TXN

Texas Parks and Wildlife Magazine
Austin   TX
1942 -
Type: 4 Frequency: 2
Earlier Title: Texas Game and Fish
IGA, IXA, IYU, TXN

Texas Sports
Houston   TX
1979 - Unkwn
Type: 4 Frequency: 5
IGA, IXA, IYU, TXN

Texas Sportsman
San Antonio   TX
1976 - Unkwn
Type: 4 Frequency: 3
IXA

Texas Sportsworld
City unknown   TX
1985 - Unkwn
Type: 4 Frequency: 2
IGA, IXA, IYU, TXA

Texas Tennis
Waco   TX
1957 - Unkwn
Type: 4 Frequency: Unkwn
IYU, TPN, TXR

Texas Vision
Dallas   TX
1977 -
Type: 2 Frequency: 2
Earlier Title: Vision (Dallas)
IGA, TXA, IYU

Texas Woman
Dallas   TX
1979 - 1980
Type: 4 Frequency: 2
IXA, SAP, TAP, TXG

Third Coast Magazine, The Magazine of Austin
Austin   TX
1981 - 1987
Type: 1 Frequency: 2
Earlier Title: Third Coast: The
Magazine of Contemporary Austin
IXA, IYU, TXG

This Alaska
Anchorage   AK
1968 -
Type: 2 Frequency: 4

This Is West Texas
City unknown   TX
1920 - Unkwn
Type: 2 Frequency: Unkwn

This Month in Ann Arbor
Ann Arbor   MI
1984 -
Type: 1 Frequency: 3

This Week in Denver
Denver   CO
1984 - Unkwn
Type: 1 Frequency: 2
COP, DPL, UUM, WYU

Tidewater Life
Hampton   VA
1978 - Unkwn
Type: 2 Frequency: 3

Topeka Magazine
Topeka   KS
1974 - Unkwn
Type: 1 Frequency: 2

Town & Gown Magazine
State College   PA
1966 - Unkwn
Type: 1 Frequency: 2
UPM

Town and Country Journal
Roulette   PA
1972 - Unkwn
Type: 2 Frequency: 2

Town Crier
East Brunswick   NJ
Unkwn - Unkwn
Type: 1 Frequency: Unkwn

Town Squire
Kansas City   MO
1968 - 1987
Type: 1 Frequency: 2
Earlier Title: Kansas City Magazine

Townsfolk
Chicago   IL
1928 -
Type: 1 Frequency: 2

Trenton Magazine
Trenton   NJ
1924 - 1979
Type: 1 Frequency: 2
JNA, NJL, RID

Triad
Greensboro   NC
1976 - 1978
Type: 1 Frequency: 3
EWF, NGU

*Tropical Living Homemaker and
Gardener*
Miami   FL
1950 - 1964
Type: 4 Frequency: 3
FDA, FHM, FUG

True West
Austin   TX
1953 -
Type: 4 Frequency: 3
DLC, BGU, TKN, IXA, IYU, VPI

Tucson Lifestyle Magazine
Tucson   AZ
1982 -
Type: 1 Frequency: 2
AZT, AZU

Tucson Magazine
Tucson   AZ
1975 -
Type: 1 Frequency: 3
Earlier Title: Desert Silhouette's
Tucson
AZT, AZU, DPL

Tulsa Magazine
Tulsa   OK
1959 -
Type: 1 Frequency: 2
OKX

Twin Cities
Minneapolis   MN
1978 -
Type: 1 Frequency: 2
DLC, DUD, MNJ, MPI, NYP

Twin Cities
Minneapolis   MN
1963 - 1969
Type: Unkwn Frequency: 2
AZS, MHS M, PI

Ulster: A Regional Magazine
New Paltz   NY
1984 -
Type: 2 Frequency: 4
VIO

Ultra
Houston   TX
1981 -
Type: 2 Frequency: 2
DLC, IXA, IYU, TXR

Update Magazine
Cranston   RI
Unkwn -
Type: 2 Frequency: 2

Urban West
San Francisco   CA
1967 - Unkwn
Type: 2 Frequency: 3
CLU, CSJ, LPU, DLC

Utah Holiday Magazine
Salt Lake City   UT
1971 -
Type: 2 Frequency: 2
ULC, UUM, UUO

Utah Life
Salt Lake City   UT
1975 - Unkwn
Type: 2 Frequency: 2

Utah Magazine
Salt Lake City   UT
1974 - Unkwn
Type: 2 Frequency: 3

Vail Magazine
Denver   CO
1976 -
Type: 1 Frequency: 4
DPL

Valley Life Magazine
Tarzana   CA
1983 - Unkwn
Type: 2 Frequency: 3

Valley Magazine
Granada Hills   CA
1976 -
Type: 2 Frequency: 2
CNO, LPU

Valley Monthly
Allentown   PA
1976 - Unkwn
Type: 2 Frequency: 2

Valley Monthly Magazine
Middletown   PA
1976 -
Type: 2 Frequency: 2

Valley Traveller, The
Allentown   PA
1965 - Unkwn
Type: 2 Frequency: 2

Ventura County Magazine
Thousand Oaks   CA
1982 -
Type: 2 Frequency: 3

Veranda, A Gallery of Southern Style
Atlanta   GA
1987 -
Type: 4 Frequency: 4
NNM

Vermont Dining & Hospitality
City unknown   VT
1983 - 1985
Type: 2 Frequency: 5

Vermont Life Magazine
Montpelier   VT
1946 -
Type: 2 Frequency: 4
DLC, VTU

Vermont Quarterly
City   VT
1985 - Unkwn
Type: 2 Frequency: 5
UCW, DLC, NHM, VTU

Vermont Woman
Burlington   VT
1985 -
Type: 4 Frequency: 2
VTT, VTU

Victor Valley Magazine
Victorville   CA
1982 -
Type: 2 Frequency: 3

Vida/Miami
Miami   FL
1981 - Unkwn
Type: 3 Frequency: 2

View of Puget Sound
Seattle   WA
Unkwn - Unkwn
Type: 2 Frequency: 2

View Northwest
Bellevue   WA
1973 - Unkwn
Type: 2 Frequency: 2

Virginia Cardinal; The Magazine of Northern Virginia
Vienna   VA
1971 - 1975
Type: 2 Frequency: 2
VAX, VGM, VIC

Virginia Cavalcade
Richmond   VA
1951 -
Type: 4 Frequency: 4
DLC, KUK, NYP, VA@, VPI

Virginia Country
Berryville   VA
1979 -
Type: 2 Frequency: 3
Earlier Title: Virginia Hunt Country
DLC, VA@, VIC, VWM

Virginia Forests Magazine
Richmond   VA
1946 -
Type: 4 Frequency: 4
FUA, GUA, VA@, VPI

Virginia Lifestyle
Richmond   VA
1974 - 1979
Type: 2 Frequency: 2
Earlier Title: Richmond Lifestyle
VIC, VLW, VRC, VRU

Virginia Wildlife
Richmond   VA
1920 -
Type: 4 Frequency: 2
AAA, DLC, RIU, VA@, VPI, VRU

Virginian, The
New Hope   VA
1979 -
Type: 2 Frequency: 3
Earlier Title: Shenandoah Valley
DLC, VPI

Viva New Mexico
Albuquerque   NM
1980 - 1980
Type: 2 Frequency: 3
IQU, IRU, UUM

Washington Dossier
Washington   DC
1975 -
Type: 1 Frequency: 2
DLC, NYP, VAX

Washington Fishing Holes
Burlington   WA
1974 -
Type: 4 Frequency: 2
WAU

Washington Monthly
Washington   DC
1969 -
Type: Unkwn Frequency: 2
AAA, LPU, DGU, DGW, DLC, NYP

Washington Woman, The
Arlington   VA
1984 -
Type: 3 Frequency: 2
DLC, NYP, AXL

Washington World
Washington   DC
1961 - 1966
Type: Unkwn Frequency: 2
Earlier Title: World
CLU, SOI, VA@

*Washington; The Evergreen State
Magazine*
Seattle   WA
1984 -
Type: 2 Frequency: 5
NYP, TAW, WAU

Washingtonian
Washington   DC
1965 -
Type: 1 Frequency: 2
DGU, DGW, DLC, NYP, VPI

Waterbury Woman
Hamden   CT
1987 -
Type: 3 Frequency: 2

*Waterfront Magazine, Southern
California's Boating News*
Newport Beach   CA
1979 -
Type: 4 Frequency: 2

Weekly: Seattle's Newsmagazine
Seattle   WA
1976 - 1977
Type: 3 Frequency: 1
Earlier Title: Weekly of Metropol-
itan Seattle
WAU

West
Las Vegas   NV
1956 - Unkwn
Type: 2 Frequency: 4

West Florida Life
Sarasota   FL
1983 - Unkwn
Type: 2 Frequency: 3

West Michigan Magazine
Grand Rapids   MI
1971 -
Type: 2 Frequency: 2
Earlier Title: Accent/Grand Rap-
ids
EEX, EXG, EXR

West Virginia Conservation
Charleston   WV
1937 - 1967
Type: 4 Frequency: 2
MNP, WAU

West Virginia Hills & Streams
Durbin   WV
1970 - Unkwn
Type: 4 Frequency: 2

West Virginia Woodsman
Martinsburg   WV
1984 -
Type: 4 Frequency: 4

West, The
Freeport   NY
1964 - Unkwn
Type: 2 Frequency: 2
AZU, DPL, IRU, UUM

Westchester Illustrated
Yonkers   NY
1976 - Unkwn
Type: 2 Frequency: 2
NYD, VVS

Westchester Magazine
Mamaruneck   NY
1969 - 1982
Type: 2 Frequency: 2
Earlier Title: Country Life Magazine
NYC, NYD, VVS

Western & California Visitor
Los Angeles   CA
1954 - Unkwn
Type: 2 Frequency: 2

Western Boatman, The
Gardena   CA
1983 -
Type: 4 Frequency: 3

Western Homes and Living
City unknown
Unkwn - Unkwn
Type: 4 Frequency: Unkwn

Western Massachusetts Magazine
Northampton   MA
1983 -
Type: 2 Frequency: 3
Earlier Title: Country Side
AUM

Western Outdoors
Costa Mesa   CA
1960 -
Type: 4 Frequency: 2
DPL, OSE, OSO

Western Reserve Magazine
North Canton   OH
1973 -
Type: 2 Frequency: 2
DLC, KSU, OHT, YNG

Western RV Traveler
Alemeda   CA
1978 -
Type: 4 Frequency: 2
Earlier Title: California Traveler

Western Ski Time
San Francisco   CA
1964 - Unkwn
Type: 4 Frequency: 5
LPU

Western Skier
San Francisco   CA
1963 - Unkwn
Type: 4 Frequency: 3
Earlier Title: Far West Skier

Westways
Los Angeles   CA
1909 -
Type: 2 Frequency: 2
AZS, AZU, CDS, CFI, CIT

Where Magenzine
New York   NY
1934 -
Type: 1 Frequency: 2

Wichitan
Wichita   KS
1978 - 1985
Type: 1 Frequency: 2
DLC, KKN, KSW

Wildlife in North Carolina
Raleigh   NC
1937 -
Type: 4 Frequency: 5
Earlier Title: North Carolina Wildlife
DLC, NYP, NRC

Window of New Hampshire
Londondury   VT
1970 - Unkwn
Type: 2 Frequency: 2

Window of Vermont Magazine
Woodstock   VT
1982 -
Type: 2 Frequency: 3
VTU

Windy City Sports
Wilmette   IL
1986 -
Type: 3 Frequency: 5

Winston-Salem Magazine
Winston-Salem   NC
1984 -
Type: 1 Frequency: 3
EWF

Wisconsin Athlete
Madison   WI
1981 -
Type: 4 Frequency: 2
GZD, WIH

Wisconsin Monthly
Brookfield   WI
1982 -
Type: 2 Frequency: 2
WIH

Wisconsin Regional
Madison   WI
1979 -
Type: 2 Frequency: 2
CGP, WIH, WIM

Wisconsin Silent Sports
Waupaca   WI
1984 -
Type: 4 Frequency: 2
GZD, WIH

Wisconsin Sportsman
Oshkosh   WI
1972 -
Type: 4 Frequency: 3
DLC, GZD, WIH

Wisconsin Trails; the Magazine of Wisconsin
Madison   WI
1959 -
Type: 2 Frequency: 3
Earlier Title: Wisconsin Tales & Trails
LPU, EXW, MHS, GZD

Wisconsonite, The
Marshall   WI
1961 - Unkwn
Type: 2 Frequency: 2
WIM, WIW

Wisdom's Child
NewYork   NY
1969 - Unkwn
Type: 1 Frequency: Unkwn

Wonderful West Virginia
Charleston   WV
1936 -
Type: 2 Frequency: 2
AAA, DLC, NYP, VPI, WVT, WVU

Wonderful World of Ohio
Columbus   OH
1965 - Unkwn
Type: 2 Frequency: 2
DPL, SOI, COO, BGU, OHI

Wyoming
Casper   WY
1983 - Unkwn
Type: 2 Frequency: 2
WYU

Wyoming Wildlife
Cheyenne   WY
1936 -
Type: 4 Frequency: 2
ALM, KUK, NRC, WYU

Yankee
Dublin   NH
1935 -
Type: 2 Frequency: 2
AAA, DLC, NHM, NYP, VPI

Yankee Homes
Dublin   NH
1985 -
Type: 4 Frequency: 2
FRP, FRF

99 Miles of River Magazine
Cincinnati   OH
Unkwn - Unkwn
Type: 4 Frequency: 5

Part II

Chronological List of Regional Interest Magazine Titles, 1950-1988 (Arranged alphabetically by state)

1888

Paradise of the Pacific Magazine

1898

*Sunset; the Magazine of Western
    Living*

1900

*Bostonia, The Magazine of Culture
    & Ideas*

1906

Baltimore Magazine
Palm Beach Life
Santa Barbara

1908

Greater Philadelphia Magazine
Philadelphia Magazine

1909

Westways

1915

Midwest Motorist, The

1918

Michigan Living

1920

Miamian, The
Shreveport
This Is West Texas
Virginia Wildlife

1921

Chronicles of Oklahoma, The
Miami/South Florida Magazine

1922

Dallas Magazine
Nebraskaland

1923

New Mexico Magazine
New Yorker, The

1924

Duluthian, The
Maryland Conservationist
Trenton Magazine

1925

Arizona Highways
*Mountain Life and Work; Magazine
    of the Appalachian South*
Park Avenue Social Review

1928

Arizona Wildlife Sportsman
Townsfolk

1929

Greater Lubbock Magazine

1930

Outdoor California
Pennsylvania Game News

1931

*Key Magazine/This Week in
    Pittsburgh*
Michigan Conservation
*Michigan Natural Resources Maga-
    zine*
New Jersey Life
Pennsylvania Angler

1932

Cue/New York

1933

Buffalo
*State; Down Home in North
    Carolina*

1934

Commonwealth Magazine
Outdoor Indiana
Where Magenzine

1935

*Alaska; Magazine of Life on the
    Last Frontier*
Yankee

1936

Alabama Magazine
Forest Notes
Nevada Magazine
South; the News Magazine of Dixie
Texas Parade
Wonderful West Virginia
Wyoming Wildlife

1937

In Kentucky
Mississippi Game & Fish
South Carolina Magazine
Tennessee Conservationist
West Virginia Conservation
Wildlife in North Carolina

1938

Long Island Forum
Missouri Conservationist
North Dakota Outdoors

1940

*Park East: The Magazine of New
    York*

1942

Scenic Southwest
Texas Parks and Wildlife Magazine

1943

*Rayburn's Ozark Guide; The
    Magazine of the Ozarks*

1944

Houston Town & Country Magazine
Scenic South

1945

Chicago History
Isle Camera, The
Kansas!
Kentucky Happy Hunting Ground

Outdoor Oklahoma
Rural Georgia

1946

Arkansas Sportsman
Cape Cod Guide
Lakeland Boating
Maine Life Magazine
New South
Orlando Magazine
Orlando-Land Magazine
Rural Arkansas Magazine
Rural Living
Scenic Idaho
Vermont Life Magazine
Virginia Forests Magazine

1947

Exclusively Yours, Wisconsin
Florida Wildlife
Michigan Out-of-Doors
Rural Electric Nebraskan

1948

El Paso Magazine
Hawaiian Sportsman
Idaho Wildlife Review
Louisiana Conservationist
Rural Kentuckian
Rural Missouri
San Diego Magazine

1949

Cape Cod Compass
Colorado Wonderland
Faulkner Facts and Fiddlings
*Frontier; The Voice of the New
    West*
New England Living
Southern Gardening

1950

Bronx Westchester Life
Enchantment Magazine
Lancaster Magazine
Living in South Carolina
Louisville Magazine
Montana Outdoors
Montana Wildlife
New Jersey Outdoors
*Tropical Living Homemaker and
    Gardener*

1951

Bay Window
Great Lakelands, The
Long Island Home
Montana; the Magazine of Western
    History
New Hampshire Profiles
Virginia Cavalcade

1952

Chicago
Chicago Guide
Colorado Outdoors
Florida Explorer
Historic Bucks County
Iowan, The
INFO
New Haven INFO Magazine
Ozarks Mountaineer
Rural Montana

1953

Inland; The Magazine of the Mid-
    dle West
Palm Beach Social Pictorial
San Francisco Focus
Southern Outdoors Magazine
Texas Highways Magazine
True West

1954

Boston
California & Western Visitor
Coast Magazine
Down East Magazine
Fairfield County Magazine
New Norfolk Magazine
North Dakota REC Magazine
Northwest Ruralite
Ruralite
South Carolina Wildlife
Western & California Visitor

1955

Southern Golfer

1956

Greater Portland Magazine
Milwaukee
New Mexico Wildlife
Oklahoma Today

Old Florida Cracker
West

1957

Beacon Magazine of Hawaii
Feather River Territorial
Georgia Magazine
Idaho Yesterdays
Orange County Magazine
San Fernando Valley
San Francisco Magazine
Southern Bowler
Texas Tennis

1958

Bucks County Panorama Magazine
Delta Review (Jackson)
Delta Review (Memphis)
Delta Review (New Orleans)
Detroit Skyliner
Dimension-Cincinnati
Kalamazoo
Los Angeles FM & Fine Arts
New York Running News
Palm Springs Life
Playground of the Rockies
Tennessee Magazine

1959

Louisiana Magazette
New England Galaxy
New Orleanian
Panorama, The Magazine of Bucks
    County
Pennsylvania Sportsman
Point West
Tulsa Magazine
Wisconsin Trails; the Magazine of
    Wisconsin

1960

Austin Magazine
Bucks County Life
Californian
Carolina Golfer
Carolina Sportsman
Chicago Scene
Coast Magazine
Eastern Tennis
Los Angeles; the Magazine of
    Southern California
Pacific Scene
Southern Gardens

Western Outdoors

1961

Atlanta Magazine
Birmingham
Central New Yorker
Four Corners
Gondolier, Florida's Boating Mag-
    azine
Southern Waterways
Southwesterner
Washington World
Wisconsonite, The

1962

Boston Magazine
Corvallis Magazine
Delaware Today Magazine
Focus/Midwest
Four Corner Wonder Land Maga-
    zine
Ft Lauderdale Magazine
Georgia Outdoors
Hawaii U S A
Hoosierland Magazine
Illinois Magazine, The Magazine of
    the Prairie State
Indianapolis Magazine
Mississippi News and Views
Orange County Illustrated
Rural Vermonter

1963

Baltimore Scene
Jacksonville Magazine
Kalamazoo Magazine
Nashville Magazine
Omnibus and Chicago FM Guide
St Louis Magazine
Twin Cities
Western Skier

1964

American West
Brown Texan
Dayton Magazine
Dayton USA
Golden West
Grand Rapids Magazine
Greater Indianapolis
Kentucky Golfer
Minnesota Monthly
New Magazine

Old West
Outdoor Arizona
Park East
Ranch & Coast: The Magazine of
    the California Riviera
Seattle Magazine
South Illustrated
Spotlighting Nebraska
West, The
Western Ski Time

1965

Colorful Colorado
Florida's Gold Coast
Madison Select
Pictorial Life; The Society Journal
    of the Gold Coast
Surfing East
Texas Metro; Magazine of Texas
    Living
Valley Traveller, The
Washingtonian
Wonderful World of Ohio

1966

Arkansas State Magazine
Augusta Magazine
Colorado Magazine
Colorado/Rocky Mountain West
Florida Profile; Sunshine State
    Panorama
Honolulu
Indianapolis Downtowner
Maine Digest
New Orleans Magazine
Nor'westing
Ohio Fisherman
Outdoors in Georgia
Pacific Northwest
Phoenix Magazine
Southern Living
Southwest Skier
Town & Gown Magazine

1967

Atlanta Skier
Buffalo Spree Magazine
Cincinnati Magazine
City Magazine
Dixie Golf
High Country, The
Midwest Outdoors
Oregon Outdoors
Pennsylvania Heritage

Urban West

1968

Ark/Ozark
Atlanta Arts
Charlotte Magazine
Charlotte Metrolina Magazine
Desert Magazine
Florida Golfer
Florida Sportsman
Hoosier Outdoors
Kansas City Town Squire
Lynchburg
Maryland Magazine
Missouri Highways
Missouri; The Harbinger Magazine
New York Magazine
Northeast Outdoors
Sandlapper; The Magazine of
   South Carolina
This Alaska
Town Squire

1969

Acadiana Profile; A Magazine for
   Bi-lingual Louisiana
Alaska Magazine
Of Westchester Magazine
Pittsburgh Magazine
Raleigh
Savannah Magazine
Southeast Ohio
Southern Golf
Washington Monthly
Westchester Magazine
Wisdom's Child

1970

Adirondack Life
Arizona Living
California Journal
Denver
Denver Magazine
Fiesta Magazine
Great Lakes Sportsman
Gulfshore Life Magazine
Metro, The Magazine of South-
   eastern Virginia
Montana Magazine
Montana West: Magazine of the
   Northern Rockies
Mountain Living
New England Senior Citizen
New Hampshire Echoes

New Worlds
Rockies Magazine, The
Sports West
West Virginia Hills & Streams
Window of New Hampshire

1971

A P T (Austin People Today)
Alaska Journal
Austin People Today
Chesapeake Bay Magazine
Connecticut Magazine
Golden Gate North
Houston Monthly
Louisiana Woods & Water
Northern Virginian
On the Sound
Oregon Magazine
Oregon Times Magazine
Pacifica Magazine
Southwest Art
Utah Holiday Magazine
Virginia Cardinal; The Magazine
   of Northern Virginia
West Michigan Magazine

1972

Accent West
Alaska Geographic
Ann Arbor Scene Magazine
Bend of the River Magazine
Borrowed Times
Brown's Guide to Georgia
Chicago Reporter, The
Cleveland Magazine
Colorado Express, The
Connecticut Fireside
Dallas/Fort Worth Living
Denver Monthly
Greatlakes
High Country
Houston Scene Magazine
Hudson Valley Magazine
Indian River Life
LI Magazine
MPLS--St Paul Magazine
New England Bride
New England Messenger
Northwest Experience
On The Shore
Santa Fean
Southern Boating Magazine
Town and Country Journal
Wisconsin Sportsman

1973

Appalachian Heritage
Central Florida Magazine
Chicagoan
Coastline Magazine
Delta Scene
Florida Life
Great Lakes Fisherman
Great Lakes Gazette
Houston Living
Hyde Parker Magazine
Maine Antique Digest
Midwest World
Minnesotan
Missouri Life
Nashville!
New East; Magazine of Eastern
    North Carolina
Northwest Golfer
Pacific Wilderness Journal
Potomac Appalachian
Salt Magazine
Sioux City Magazine
Southern Exposure
Texas Fisherman
Texas Monthly
View Northwest
Western Reserve Magazine

1974

Arkansas Times
Austin Living
Blair & Ketchum's Country Journal
Broward Life
BFLO
Capital Magazine
City Magazine
D Magazine
Denver Living
Empire State Report
Georgia Life
Hampton Life
Houston Home & Garden
Houston Metropolitan Magazine
Long Island Sportsman
Michigan Historical Review
Ocooch Mountain News; A Maga-
    zine of Southwest Wisconsin
Orange Coast Magazine, The Mag-
    azine of Orange County
Pacific Skipper
Pasadena Magazine
Portland
Richmond Magazine
Roanoker, The

Snowmobile West
South Magazine, The
Southern Voices
Southlander; Magazine of the His-
    toric South
Stratton-Bromley Magazine
Topeka Magazine
Utah Magazine
Virginia Lifestyle
Washington Fishing Holes

1975

Avenue M
Broome County Living
Charleston Magazine
Chicago Independent Magazine
Coastal Magazine
Columbus Monthly
Country Magazine, The
Florida Golfweek
Illinois Issues
Mountainwest Magazine
Newmonth: The Good Life in Up-
    per Wisconsin
Northwest America
Peninsula Magazine
Sacramento Magazine
Southern California Sports Guide
Tucson Magazine
Utah Life
Washington Dossier

1976

Alburquerque Singles Magazine
Ann Arbor Observer
Avenue
California
Cascades East
Colorado Woman
East-Side Express
Georgia Sportsman
Houston Northwest Magazine
Inland Empire
Kansas City Magazine
Las Vegan
Memphis
Metropolitan Beaumont
Naples Now
New Jersey Monthly
Northern Arizona Scenes
Offshore, New England's Boating
    Magazine
Omaha Magazine
Pacific Magazine
Pennsylvania Illustrated

Playsure Magazine
San Gabriel Valley Magazine
Sarasota Town & Country Magazine
Sedona Life
Susquehanna Monthly Magazine
Texas Sportsman
Triad
Vail Magazine
Valley Magazine
Valley Monthly
Valley Monthly Magazine
Weekly: Seattle's Newsmagazine
Westchester Illustrated

1977

Aloha, The Magazine of Hawaii and
    the Pacific
Atlanta Singles Magazine &
    Datebook
Atlantic City Magazine
Back Home in Kentucky
Bay Views; Reflecting the Good
    Life of the Golden Gate
Cumberland
Detroiter, The
Eastern Outdoors
Florida Monthly
Fort Collins Magazine
Gulf Coast Fisherman
Houston City Magazine
Indianapolis at Home
Indianapolis Monthly
Inland Shores
Jackson Magazine
Mesa Magazine
Minnesota Sportsman
North Shore, the Magazine for
    Living on the Gold Coast
Off P'Tree
Ohio Magazine
People of North Carolina
Pittsburgher Magazine
Plainswoman
Quality of Life in Loisaida; the
    Lower East Side Magazine
Seacoast Woman
Southern Accents
Southwest Magazine
Spokane Magazine
Spotlight on Harrison
Spotlight on Mamaroneck
Spotlight on Rye
Springfield/Hartford
St Joseph Magazine
Tampa Bay Magazine

Tar Heel; The Magazine of North
    Carolina
Texas Homes
Texas Vision

1978

Alaska Outdoors
Bay Life Magazine
City
Coast Magazine
Columbiana
County Lines
Dallas-Fort Worth Home & Garden
Detroit Monthly
Florida Keys Magazine
G, Golden Triad
High Country Living Magazine
K S Magazine
L A West
Madison Magazine
Monthly Detroit
New Brooklyn
New England Running
New Texas
North Shore; the Magazine of
    Chicago's Northern Suburbs
Now in Stark County
Panorama Magazine
S. A.
San Antonio Living
South Bay Magazine
Southwest Profile
Tidewater Life
Twin Cities
Western RV Traveler
Wichitan

1979

Arkansan
Arkansas Fisherman
Austin Arts & Leisure
Boston Monthly, The
Cape Cod Life
Colorado Sportstyles Magazine
Colorado Springs Monthly
Corpus Christi Magazine
Dallas Digest
Delaware Monthly
East End Magazine
Erie Magazine
Florida Gulf Coast Living Magazine
Humboldt County Magazine
Lake Superior Magazine
Marblehead Magazine; A Seacoast
    Journal

Milwaukee Magazine
Monterey Life
New Black South
New England Racquet Sport
New York's Nightlife
Orange County Home & Garden
Orange County Magazine
Phoenix Living
Ports South
Richmond Lifestyle
Rocky Mountain Magazine
San Diego Home/Garden
Sarasota
Saratoga - The Magazine
South Jersey
Southern Partisan
Southern World
Springfield! Magazine
Tallahassee Magazine
Texas Sports
Texas Woman
Virginia Country
Virginian, The
Waterfront Magazine, Southern
    California's Boating News
Wisconsin Regional

1980

Alabama Game & Fish
Alabama Monthly
Augusta Spectator
Austin Homes & Gardens
Capital Shopper: The Magazine
    That Pays for Itself
Chicago Mahogany
Chicago Sports Scene
Colorado Homes & Lifestyles
Colorado Sports Monthly
Connecticut Travels
Donde
East-West Magazine
Georgia Journal
Gloucester: The Magazine of the
    New England Coast
Knoxville Lifestyle
Los Angeles Home and Garden
Miami Mensual
Michigan Environs
Mid-Atlantic Country Magazine
Museums New York
New England Sampler
New Jersey Shore Magazine
Northern Ohio Live
Phoenix Home & Garden
Queen City
Scottsdale Magazine

South Florida Outdoors
Southwest Woman
Susquehanna Valley
Tampa/St Petersburg
Tennessee Sportsman
Viva New Mexico

1981

Atlanta Impressions
Atlantic City Express
Bakersfield Lifestyle Magazine
Boca Raton Magazine
Boulevards, The Magazine of San
    Francisco
California Angler
Carolina Game and Fish
Champaign-Urbana Magazine
City Limits
Elite Magazine, The Southwest
    Features/Society Magazine
Greenville Magazine
Hartford Woman
House in the Hamptons
Long Island's Night Life
Louisiana Game & Fish
Louisiana Life
Mississippi Sportsman
New Bedford Magazine
New Florida
New York Alive
North Shore Life Magazine
Pacific Life
Pennsylvania Magazine
Politics New England
River Cities; the Magazine of
    Shreveport and Bossier
San Antonio Monthly
Senior, California Senior's Maga-
    zine
Sierra Life Magazine, The Maga-
    zine of the High Sierra
South Florida Living
Tahoe Today
Texas Gardener
Texas Hill Country Scenes
Third Coast Magazine, The Maga-
    zine of Austin
Ultra
Vida/Miami
Wisconsin Athlete

1982

Alaska Woman
Beverly Hills World
Black New Orleans

Blvd
Carolina Lifestyle
City Guide, Broadway Magazine
Columbus Magazine
Country Life Magazine
Empire Sports Magazine
G The Magazine of Gainesville
Goodlife
Hartford
High Country Magazine
Indian River Lifestyle
Island Life
Life & Home
Long Island Life
Metropolis; The Architecture and
    Design Magazine of New York
Michigan Golfer
Mississippi Magazine
Mississippi; A View of the
    Magnolia State
New Haven
New South Magazine, The
New York Habitat, For Co-op,
    Condominium and Loft Living
Northcoast View
Oklahoma City Metro
Oklahoma Home & Lifestyle
Oregon Coast
Parkway, The Magazine for New
    North Dallas
Pennsylvania Outdoors
Princeton Magazine
San Francisco Goodlife
Southeastern
Tucson Lifestyle Magazine
Ventura County Magazine
Victor Valley Magazine
Window of Vermont Magazine
Wisconsin Monthly

1983

Arizona Arts & Travel
Austin Woman
Beverly Hills
California Homes and Lifestyles
Center Magazine
Coastal Journal
Colorado Art Scene
Columbia Review
Connecticut Riding
Erie & Chantauqua Magazine
Fairfield County Woman
Gulf Coast Golfer
Houston Goodlife
Huckleberry: Magazine for the
    New River Valley

Hudson Valley Living
Kentucky Dossier
Manhattan Magazine
Mountain Magazine
New York Sports
Northwest Living
Oklahoma Game & Fish
Orange County Gentry
Orlando Monthly
San Angelo Magazine
San Diego Woman
Sara Bay Monthly
Scottsdale Scene Magazine
Seattle Woman, The Magazine with
    a New View
Single Life Milwaukee
Southern Bodybuilder
Southern Homes
Tampa Bay Metro Magazine
Tempo Magazine; Life in North-
    eastern Pennsylvania
Valley Life Magazine
Vermont Dining & Hospitality
West Florida Life
Western Boatman, The
Western Massachusetts Magazine
Wyoming

1984

Arizona Golf Journal
Atlantic City Night Life
Boat Pennsylvania
Buffalo Scene Magazine
Chicago Life
Coast & County
Columbus Homes & Lifestyles
Florida Living
Golden State
Hawaii Profile
Houstonian Magazine
Indianapolis Woman
La Jolla
Magazine of Utah, The
Malibu
Manhattan, inc
Mauian Magazine
Metropolitan Detroit
Michigan Woman
New England Living
New England Monthly
New Haven County Woman
New York Image
Newport Beach
North Florida Living
North Georgia Journal
Northshore Magazine

O Magazine
Right Here, The Hometown Magazine
RSVP, The Magazine of Good Living
San Antonio Today
South Florida Home & Garden
Southern Star
Sportswise Philadelphia
St George Magazine
This Month in Ann Arbor
This Week in Denver
Ulster: A Regional Magazine
Washington Woman, The
Washington; The Evergreen State Magazine
West Virginia Woodsman
Winston-Salem Magazine
Wisconsin Silent Sports

1985

Above the Bridge Magazine
Capital Region Magazine
Connecticut Country Life
Connecticut's Finest
Grapevine's Finger Lakes Magazine
Jacksonville Today
L A Style
L A Woman
Mobile Bay Monthly
Myrtle Beach Magazine
Peninsula
San Antonio Homes & Gardens
Seacoast Life
Southern Vermont Magazine
Texas Sportsworld
Vermont Quarterly
Vermont Woman
Yankee Homes

1986

Boston Woman
City-County Magazine
Colorado Outdoor Journal
Fishing and Hunting Journal: Magazine of the Ozark Region
Garden State Home & Garden
Great Lakes Travel & Living
Kansas City Homes & Gardens
Macon Magazine
Metro
Miami Skier
New Charlotte Magazine
New England Getaways
New Jersey Home & Garden

New York Family
New York Woman
North Texas Golfer
Northern Adventures Magazine; a Magazine on Alaska
Peninsula Magazine
Rhode Island Woman
Rockford Magazine
Southern Magazine
Tampa Bay--The Suncoast Magazine
Windy City Sports

1987

Albuquerque Senior Scene Magazine
Arizona Monthly
Chicago Times
Domain
Fairfax
Great Lakes Sailor
Greenville Woman
Highlands of the Virginias Magazine
Images of Hampton Roads
Inside Chicago
Lake Country
Louisiana Journal
Metropolitan: Toledo and the Northcoast
Midwest Living, A Celebration of the Heartland
New Dominion
New York Lifestyles
Northern California Home & Garden
Northfield Magazine, The
Plantation Monthly
San Francisco: The Magazine
Southern Style
Southern Travel
Veranda, A Gallery of Southern Style
Waterbury Woman

1988

Angeles
Blue Ridge Country
California Basketball
Cola. The Magazine of Columbia
Hartford Monthly
Long Island Monthly
Lynchburg All-American
Mississippi Coast
Monroe

New Hampshire Spirit
Oh! Idaho
Pleasant Hawaii
Prosperous Times
Rhode Island Monthly
Southern Bride
Tampa Bay Life
Tampa Bay New Homes
Tennessee Illustrated

Founding date unknown

All Florida Magazine
Atlantic Coastal Diver
Big Valley, The San Fernando
    Valley Magazine
Bittersweet, The Flavor of
    Northcountry Living
Chicago Omnibus
Chicagoland
City Limits, News for the the
    Other New York
City Magazine
Coral Springs Monthly
Detroit and Suburban Life
DM: Des Moines' Metropolitan
    Magazine
Florida Lifestyle
Fort Wayne
Galveston Monthly Magazine
Gentry Magazine, The Magazine
    of Orange County People
H Magazine
Hartford County Woman
High Country
Hingham Town Crier
Houston Woman
In New York Magazine
Island Monthly Reader, The
Kansas City Woman

Kansas Game and Fish
Lansing Magazine
Linking the Dots
Louisiana Magazine
Louisiana: This Month
Magazine of Cambridge
Maine
Midwest Mariner
Milwaukee Impressions
New Californian
New Chicago
New England Sports
New England Sportsman
New Jersey Living
New Vistas
Newark
Nightbeat Magazine
Northeast Magazine
Ohio River Magazine
Okc
Oklahoma Living Magazine
Omaha Profile
Palm Beach Illustrated
Palm Springs Villager
Peachtree Magazine
Posh
Sam Houston's Metropolitan Maga-
    zine
Ski South, The Magazine of
    Southern Skiers
South Carolina History Illustrated
Southern California Living
Syracuse Magazine
Tally
Town Crier
Update Magazine
View of Puget Sound
Western Homes and Living
99 Miles of River Magazine

Part III

Geographical List of Regional Interest Magazine Titles, 1950-1988

Alabama

Alabama Magazine
Alabama Monthly
Birmingham
Mobile Bay Monthly
South Illustrated
South; the News Magazine of Dixie
Southern Accents
Southern Living
Southern Outdoors Magazine
Southlander; Magazine of the Historic South

Alaska

Alaska Geographic
Alaska Journal
Alaska Magazine
Alaska Outdoors
Alaska Woman
Alaska; Magazine of Life on the Last Frontier
Northern Adventures Magazine; a Magazine on Alaska
This Alaska

Arizona

American West
Arizona Arts & Travel
Arizona Golf Journal
Arizona Highways
Arizona Living
Arizona Monthly
Arizona Wildlife Sportsman
Elite Magazine, The Southwest Features/Society Magazine
Mesa Magazine
Outdoor Arizona
Phoenix Home & Garden
Phoenix Magazine
Point West
Scenic Southwest
Scottsdale Magazine
Scottsdale Scene Magazine
Sedona Life
Tucson Lifestyle Magazine
Tucson Magazine

Arkansas

Ark/Ozark
Arkansan
Arkansas Fisherman
Arkansas State Magazine
Arkansas Times
Faulkner Facts and Fiddlings
Rayburn's Ozark Guide; The Magazine of the Ozarks
Rural Arkansas Magazine
Southern Magazine

California

Angeles
Bakersfield Lifestyle Magazine
Bay Views: Reflecting the Good Life of the Golden Gate
Bay Window
Beverly Hills
Beverly Hills World
Big Valley, The San Fernando Valley Magazine
Boulevards, The Magazine of San Francisco
California
California & Western Visitor
California Angler
California Basketball
California Homes and Lifestyles
California Journal
Californian
City Magazine
Coast Magazine
Coastline Magazine
Colorado Sportstyles Magazine
Desert Magazine
Feather River Territorial
Frontier; The Voice of the New West
Gentry Magazine, The Magazine of Orange County People
Golden Gate North
Golden State
High Country Magazine
High Country, The
Humboldt County Magazine
Inland Empire
L A Style
L A West
L A Woman
La Jolla
Los Angeles Home and Garden
Los Angeles; the Magazine of Southern California
Malibu
Metro
Monterey Life
New Californian
New Worlds
Newport Beach
Northcoast View

Northern California Home & Garden
Orange Coast Magazine, The Magazine of Orange County
Orange County Gentry
Orange County Home & Garden
Orange County Illustrated
Orange County Magazine
Orange County Magazine
Outdoor California
Pacific Life
Pacific Scene
Pacific Skipper
Pacifica Magazine
Palm Springs Life
Palm Springs Villager
Pasadena Magazine
Peninsula
Peninsula Magazine
Ranch & Coast: The Magazine of the California Riviera
Sacramento Magazine
San Diego Home/Garden
San Diego Magazine
San Diego Woman
San Fernando Valley
San Francisco Focus
San Francisco Goodlife
San Francisco Magazine
San Francisco: The Magazine
San Gabriel Valley Magazine
Santa Barbara
Senior, California Senior's Magazine
Sierra Life Magazine, The Magazine of the High Sierra
South Bay Magazine
Southern California Living
Southern California Sports Guide
Southwest Skier
Sunset; the Magazine of Western Living
Urban West
Valley Life Magazine
Valley Magazine
Ventura County Magazine
Victor Valley Magazine
Waterfront Magazine, Southern California's Boating News
Western & California Visitor
Western Boatman, The
Western Outdoors
Western RV Traveler
Western Ski Time
Western Skier
Westways

Colorado

Colorado Art Scene
Colorado Express, The
Colorado Homes & Lifestyles
Colorado Magazine
Colorado Outdoor Journal
Colorado Outdoors
Colorado Sports Monthly
Colorado Springs Monthly
Colorado Woman
Colorado Wonderland
Colorado/Rocky Mountain West
Colorful Colorado
Denver
Denver Living
Denver Magazine
Denver Monthly
Fort Collins Magazine
Four Corner Wonder Land Magazine
Mountain Magazine
Playground of the Rockies
Rocky Mountain Magazine
This Week in Denver
Vail Magazine

Connecticut

Connecticut Country Life
Connecticut Fireside
Connecticut Magazine
Connecticut Riding
Connecticut Travels
Country Life Magazine
Eastern Outdoors
Fairfield County Magazine
Fairfield County Woman
Hartford County Woman
Hartford Monthly
Hartford Woman
New Haven
New Haven County Woman
Northeast Outdoors
On The Shore
Southeastern
Tally
Waterbury Woman

Delaware

Delaware Monthly
Delaware Today Magazine

District of Columbia

Potomac Appalachian
Washington Dossier
Washington Monthly
Washington World
Washingtonian

Florida

All Florida Magazine
Bay Life Magazine
Boca Raton Magazine
Broward Life
Central Florida Magazine
Coral Springs Monthly
Donde
Florida Explorer
Florida Golfer
Florida Golfweek
Florida Gulf Coast Living Magazine
Florida Keys Magazine
Florida Life
Florida Lifestyle
Florida Living
Florida Monthly
Florida Profile; Sunshine State Panorama
Florida Sportsman
Florida Wildlife
Florida's Gold Coast
Ft Lauderdale Magazine
G The Magazine of Gainesville
Gondolier, Florida's Boating Magazine
Gulfshore Life Magazine
Indian River Life
Indian River Lifestyle
Island Life
Jacksonville Magazine
Jacksonville Today
Life & Home
Miami Mensual
Miami Skier
Miami/South Florida Magazine
Miamian, The
Naples Now
New Black South
New Florida
New Vistas
North Florida Living
Old Florida Cracker
Orlando Magazine
Orlando Monthly
Orlando-Land Magazine
Palm Beach Illustrated
Palm Beach Life

Palm Beach Social Pictorial
Pictorial Life; The Society Journal of the Gold Coast
Plantation Monthly
Sara Bay Monthly
Sarasota
Sarasota Town & Country Magazine
South Florida Home & Garden
South Florida Living
South Florida Outdoors
South Magazine, The
Southern Boating Magazine
Southern Golf
Southern Star
Southern Waterways
Tallahassee Magazine
Tampa Bay Life
Tampa Bay Magazine
Tampa Bay Metro Magazine
Tampa Bay New Homes
Tampa Bay--The Suncoast Magazine
Tampa/St Petersburg
Tropical Living Homemaker and Gardener
Vida/Miami
West Florida Life

Georgia

Alabama Game & Fish
Arkansas Sportsman
Atlanta Arts
Atlanta Impressions
Atlanta Magazine
Atlanta Singles Magazine & Datebook
Atlanta Skier
Augusta Magazine
Augusta Spectator
Brown's Guide to Georgia
Carolina Game and Fish
Coastal Magazine
Columbus Magazine
Dixie Golf
Georgia Journal
Georgia Life
Georgia Magazine
Georgia Outdoors
Georgia Sportsman
Goodlife
High Country Living Magazine
Kansas Game and Fish
Louisiana Game & Fish
Macon Magazine
Minnesota Sportsman
Mississippi Game & Fish

Mississippi Sportsman
New South
North Georgia Journal
Off P'Tree
Oklahoma Game & Fish
Outdoors in Georgia
Peachtree Magazine
Rural Georgia
Savannah Magazine
Southern Bowler
Southern Gardening
Southern Homes
Southern Voices
Tennessee Sportsman
Veranda, A Gallery of Southern
     Style

Hawaii

Aloha, The Magazine of Hawaii and
     the Pacific
Beacon Magazine of Hawaii
East-West Magazine
Hawaii Profile
Hawaii U S A
Hawaiian Sportsman
Honolulu
Mauian Magazine
Pacific Magazine
Paradise of the Pacific Magazine
Pleasant Hawaii
RSVP, The Magazine of Good Liv-
     ing

Idaho

High Country
Idaho Wildlife Review
Idaho Yesterdays
Northwest America
Northwest Experience
Oh! Idaho
Scenic Idaho
Snowmobile West

Illinois

Avenue M
Champaign-Urbana Magazine
Chicago
Chicago Guide
Chicago History
Chicago Independent Magazine
Chicago Life
Chicago Mahogany
Chicago Omnibus
Chicago Reporter, The

Chicago Scene
Chicago Sports Scene
Chicago Times
Chicagoan
Chicagoland
Greatlakes
Hyde Parker Magazine
Illinois Issues
Illinois Magazine, The Magazine of
     the Prairie State
Inland; The Magazine of the Mid-
     dle West
Inside Chicago
Lakeland Boating
Midwest Mariner
Midwest Outdoors
New Chicago
North Shore; the Magazine of
     Chicago's Northern Suburbs
Omnibus and Chicago FM Guide
Panorama Magazine
Rockford Magazine
Townsfolk
Windy City Sports

Indiana

Fort Wayne
Greater Indianapolis
Hoosier Outdoors
Hoosierland Magazine
Indianapolis at Home
Indianapolis Downtowner
Indianapolis Magazine
Indianapolis Monthly
Indianapolis Woman
Outdoor Indiana
Prosperous Times
Right Here, The Hometown Maga-
     zine

Iowa

DM: Des Moines' Metropolitan
     Magazine
Iowan, The
Midwest Living, A Celebration of
     the Heartland
Sioux City Magazine

Kansas

K S Magazine
Kansas City Homes & Gardens
Kansas City Woman
Kansas!
Topeka Magazine

Wichitan

Kentucky

Appalachian Heritage
Back Home in Kentucky
Center Magazine
In Kentucky
Kentucky Dossier
Kentucky Golfer
Kentucky Happy Hunting Ground
Louisville Magazine
Rural Kentuckian
Scenic South

Louisiana

Acadiana Profile; A Magazine for
   Bi-lingual Louisiana
Black New Orleans
Louisiana Conservationist
Louisiana Journal
Louisiana Life
Louisiana Magazette
Louisiana Magazine
Louisiana Woods & Water
Louisiana: This Month
New Orleanian
New Orleans Magazine
New South Magazine, The
Northshore Magazine
River Cities; the Magazine of
   Shreveport and Bossier
Shreveport

Maine

Bittersweet, The Flavor of
   Northcountry Living
Down East Magazine
Greater Portland Magazine
Linking the Dots
Maine
Maine Antique Digest
Maine Digest
Maine Life Magazine
New England Sampler
Salt Magazine

Maryland

Atlantic Coastal Diver
Baltimore Magazine
Baltimore Scene
Cape Cod Life
Chesapeake Bay Magazine
Maryland Conservationist

Maryland Magazine

Massachusetts

Boston
Boston Magazine
Boston Monthly, The
Boston Woman
Bostonia, The Magazine of Culture
   & Ideas
Cape Cod Compass
Cape Cod Guide
City Limits
Coast & County
Gloucester: The Magazine of the
   New England Coast
Hartford
Hingham Town Crier
Island Monthly Reader, The
Magazine of Cambridge
Marblehead Magazine; A Seacoast
   Journal
New Bedford Magazine
New England Bride
New England Galaxy
New England Getaways
New England Living
New England Living
New England Messenger
New England Monthly
New England Senior Citizen
New England Sports
North Shore Life Magazine
Offshore, New England's Boating
   Magazine
Politics New England
Springfield/Hartford
Western Massachusetts Magazine

Michigan

Above the Bridge Magazine
Ann Arbor Observer
Ann Arbor Scene Magazine
City Magazine
Detroit and Suburban Life
Detroit Monthly
Detroiter, The
Grand Rapids Magazine
Great Lakelands, The
Great Lakes Gazette
Great Lakes Sportsman
Isle Camera, The
Kalamazoo Magazine
Lansing Magazine
Metropolitan Detroit
Michigan Conservation

Michigan Environs
Michigan Golfer
Michigan Historical Review
Michigan Living
Michigan Natural Resources Maga-
    zine
Michigan Out-of-Doors
Michigan Woman
Milwaukee Impressions
Milwaukee Magazine
Monroe
Monthly Detroit
New England Sportsman
This Month in Ann Arbor
West Michigan Magazine

Minnesota

Duluthian, The
Lake Superior Magazine
Minnesota Monthly
Minnesotan
MPLS--St Paul Magazine
Northfield Magazine, The
Twin Cities
Twin Cities

Mississippi

Delta Scene
Jackson Magazine
Mississippi Coast
Mississippi Magazine
Mississippi News and Views
Mississippi; A View of the
    Magnolia State
Southern Golfer

Missouri

Blvd
City
Fishing and Hunting Journal:
    Magazine of the Ozark Region
Focus/Midwest
Kansas City Magazine
Kansas City Town Squire
Midwest Motorist, The
Missouri Conservationist
Missouri Highways
Missouri Life
Missouri; The Harbinger Magazine
Ozarks Mountaineer
Rural Missouri
Springfield! Magazine
St Joseph Magazine
St Louis Magazine

Town Squire

Montana

Borrowed Times
High Country
Montana Magazine
Montana Outdoors
Montana West: Magazine of the
    Northern Rockies
Montana Wildlife
Montana; the Magazine of Western
    History
Rural Montana

Nebraska

Nebraskaland
O Magazine
Omaha Magazine
Omaha Profile
Rural Electric Nebraskan

Nevada

Las Vegan
Nevada Magazine
Tahoe Today
West

New Hampshire

Coastal Journal
Forest Notes
New Hampshire Echoes
New Hampshire Profiles
New Hampshire Spirit
Seacoast Life
Seacoast Woman
Yankee
Yankee Homes

New Jersey

Atlantic City Magazine
Four Corners
Garden State Home & Garden
LI Magazine
New England Racquet Sport
New Jersey Home & Garden
New Jersey Life
New Jersey Living
New Jersey Monthly
New Jersey Outdoors
New Jersey Shore Magazine
Newark
Princeton Magazine

South Jersey
Surfing East
Town Crier
Trenton Magazine

New Mexico

Albuquerque Senior Scene Magazine
Alburquerque Singles Magazine
Enchantment Magazine
New Mexico Magazine
New Mexico Wildlife
Santa Fean
Southwest Magazine
Southwest Profile
Southwesterner
Viva New Mexico

New York

Adirondack Life
Atlantic City Express
Atlantic City Night Life
Avenue
Bronx Westchester Life
Broome County Living
Buffalo
Buffalo Scene Magazine
Buffalo Spree Magazine
Capital Region Magazine
Central New Yorker
City Guide, Broadway Magazine
City Limits, News for the the Other New York
City Magazine
Cue/New York
Delta Review (Jackson)
Delta Review (Memphis)
Delta Review (New Orleans)
Detroit Skyliner
Dimension-Cincinnati
East End Magazine
East-Side Express
Eastern Tennis
Empire Sports Magazine
Empire State Report
Golden West
Grapevine's Finger Lakes Magazine
Hampton Life
House in the Hamptons
Hudson Valley Living
Hudson Valley Magazine
In New York Magazine
Kalamazoo
Long Island Forum
Long Island Home

Long Island Life
Long Island Monthly
Long Island Sportsman
Long Island's Night Life
Los Angeles FM & Fine Arts
Manhattan Magazine
Manhattan, inc
Metropolis; The Architecture and Design Magazine of New York
Museums New York
New Brooklyn
New Magazine
New York Alive
New York Family
New York Habitat, For Co-op, Condominium and Loft Living
New York Image
New York Lifestyles
New York Magazine
New York Running News
New York Sports
New York Woman
New York's Nightlife
New Yorker, The
North Shore, the Magazine for Living on the Gold Coast
Of Westchester Magazine
On the Sound
Park Avenue Social Review
Park East
Park East: The Magazine of New York
Quality of Life in Loisaida; the Lower East Side Magazine
Saratoga - The Magazine
Southern Travel
Sportswise Philadelphia
Spotlight on Harrison
Spotlight on Mamaroneck
Spotlight on Rye
Syracuse Magazine
Ulster: A Regional Magazine
West, The
Westchester Illustrated
Westchester Magazine
Where Magenzine
Wisdom's Child

North Carolina

Carolina Golfer
Carolina Sportsman
Charlotte Magazine
Charlotte Metrolina Magazine
City-County Magazine
G, Golden Triad
Mountain Living

New Charlotte Magazine
New East; Magazine of Eastern
    North Carolina
People of North Carolina
Posh
Raleigh
Southern Bride
Southern Exposure
State; Down Home in North
    Carolina
Tar Heel; The Magazine of North
    Carolina
Triad
Wildlife in North Carolina
Winston-Salem Magazine

North Dakota

North Dakota Outdoors
North Dakota REC Magazine
Plainswoman

Ohio

Bend of the River Magazine
Cincinnati Magazine
Cleveland Magazine
Columbus Homes & Lifestyles
Columbus Monthly
Dayton Magazine
Dayton USA
Great Lakes Fisherman
Great Lakes Sailor
Great Lakes Travel & Living
Metropolitan: Toledo and the
    Northcoast
Midwest World
Northern Ohio Live
Now in Stark County
Ohio Fisherman
Ohio Magazine
Ohio River Magazine
Queen City
Southeast Ohio
Western Reserve Magazine
Wonderful World of Ohio
99 Miles of River Magazine

Oklahoma

Chronicles of Oklahoma, The
Okc
Oklahoma City Metro
Oklahoma Home & Lifestyle
Oklahoma Living Magazine
Oklahoma Today
Outdoor Oklahoma

Tulsa Magazine

Oregon

Cascades East
Coast Magazine
Corvallis Magazine
Northwest Ruralite
Oregon Coast
Oregon Magazine
Oregon Outdoors
Oregon Times Magazine
Pacific Wilderness Journal
Portland
Ruralite

Pennsylvania

Boat Pennsylvania
Bucks County Life
Bucks County Panorama Magazine
Country Magazine, The
County Lines
Erie & Chantauqua Magazine
Erie Magazine
Greater Philadelphia Magazine
Historic Bucks County
Key Magazine/This Week in
    Pittsburgh
Lancaster Magazine
Northeast Magazine
Panorama, The Magazine of Bucks
    County
Pennsylvania Angler
Pennsylvania Game News
Pennsylvania Heritage
Pennsylvania Illustrated
Pennsylvania Magazine
Pennsylvania Sportsman
Philadelphia Magazine
Pittsburgh Magazine
Pittsburgher Magazine
Susquehanna Monthly Magazine
Susquehanna Valley
Tempo Magazine; Life in North-
    eastern Pennsylvania
Town & Gown Magazine
Town and Country Journal
Valley Monthly
Valley Monthly Magazine
Valley Traveller, The

Rhode Island

Rhode Island Monthly
Rhode Island Woman
Update Magazine

South Carolina

Charleston Magazine
Coast Magazine
Cola. The Magazine of Columbia
Columbia Review
Greenville Magazine
Greenville Woman
Living in South Carolina
Myrtle Beach Magazine
Ports South
Sandlapper; The Magazine of
    South Carolina
South Carolina History Illustrated
South Carolina Magazine
South Carolina Wildlife
Southern Gardens
Southern Partisan
Southern World

Tennessee

Connecticut's Finest
Cumberland
Knoxville Lifestyle
Memphis
Nashville Magazine
Nashville!
Southern Bodybuilder
Southern Style
Tennessee Conservationist
Tennessee Illustrated
Tennessee Magazine

Texas

A P T (Austin People Today)
Accent West
Austin Arts & Leisure
Austin Homes & Gardens
Austin Living
Austin Magazine
Austin People Today
Austin Woman
Brown Texan
Corpus Christi Magazine
D Magazine
Dallas Digest
Dallas Magazine
Dallas-Fort Worth Home & Garden
Dallas/Fort Worth Living
Domain
El Paso Magazine
Fiesta Magazine
Galveston Monthly Magazine

Greater Lubbock Magazine
Gulf Coast Fisherman
Gulf Coast Golfer
H Magazine
Houston City Magazine
Houston Goodlife
Houston Home & Garden
Houston Living
Houston Metropolitan Magazine
Houston Monthly
Houston Northwest Magazine
Houston Scene Magazine
Houston Town & Country Magazine
Houston Woman
Houstonian Magazine
Metropolitan Beaumont
New Texas
Nightbeat Magazine
North Texas Golfer
Old West
Parkway, The Magazine for New
    North Dallas
Phoenix Living
Playsure Magazine
S. A.
Sam Houston's Metropolitan Maga-
    zine
San Angelo Magazine
San Antonio Homes & Gardens
San Antonio Living
San Antonio Monthly
San Antonio Today
Southwest Art
Southwest Woman
Texas Fisherman
Texas Gardener
Texas Highways Magazine
Texas Hill Country Scenes
Texas Homes
Texas Metro; Magazine of Texas
    Living
Texas Monthly
Texas Parade
Texas Parks and Wildlife Magazine
Texas Sports
Texas Sportsman
Texas Sportsworld
Texas Tennis
Texas Vision
Texas Woman
Third Coast Magazine, The Maga-
    zine of Austin
This Is West Texas
True West
Ultra

Utah

Magazine of Utah, The
Mountainwest Magazine
Rockies Magazine, The
Sports West
St George Magazine
Utah Holiday Magazine
Utah Life
Utah Magazine

Vermont

Blair & Ketchum's Country Journal
New England Running
Rural Vermonter
Southern Vermont Magazine
Stratton-Bromley Magazine
Vermont Dining & Hospitality
Vermont Life Magazine
Vermont Quarterly
Vermont Woman
Window of New Hampshire
Window of Vermont Magazine

Virginia

Blue Ridge Country
Capital Magazine
Capital Shopper: The Magazine
    That Pays for Itself
Carolina Lifestyle
Commonwealth Magazine
Fairfax
Highlands of the Virginias Maga-
    zine
Huckleberry: Magazine for the
    New River Valley
Images of Hampton Roads
Lake Country
Lynchburg
Lynchburg All-American
Metro, The Magazine of South-
    eastern Virginia
Mid-Atlantic Country Magazine
Mountain Life and Work; Magazine
    of the Appalachian South
New Dominion
New Norfolk Magazine
Northern Arizona Scenes
Northern Virginian
Richmond Lifestyle
Richmond Magazine
Roanoker, The
Rural Living
Ski South, The Magazine of
    Southern Skiers

Tidewater Life
Virginia Cardinal; The Magazine
    of Northern Virginia
Virginia Cavalcade
Virginia Country
Virginia Forests Magazine
Virginia Lifestyle
Virginia Wildlife
Virginian, The
Washington Woman, The

Washington

Columbiana
Nor'westing
Northwest Golfer
Northwest Living
Pacific Northwest
Peninsula Magazine
Seattle Magazine
Seattle Woman, The Magazine with
    a New View
Spokane Magazine
Spotlighting Nebraska
View of Puget Sound
View Northwest
Washington Fishing Holes
Washington; The Evergreen State
    Magazine
Weekly: Seattle's Newsmagazine

West Virginia

West Virginia Conservation
West Virginia Hills & Streams
West Virginia Woodsman
Wonderful West Virginia

Wisconsin

Exclusively Yours, Wisconsin
Inland Shores
Madison Magazine
Madison Select
Milwaukee
Newmonth: The Good Life in Up-
    per Wisconsin
Ocooch Mountain News; A Maga-
    zine of Southwest Wisconsin
Pennsylvania Outdoors
Single Life Milwaukee
Wisconsin Athlete
Wisconsin Monthly
Wisconsin Regional
Wisconsin Silent Sports
Wisconsin Sportsman

Wisconsin Trails; the Magazine of
   Wisconsin
Wisconsonite, The

Wyoming

Wyoming
Wyoming Wildlife

Appendix A

Representative List of Geographically Identified Magazines, 1743-1949 (Arranged alphabetically)

Age: Southern Eclectic Magazine
Richmond   VA
1864 - 1865

Agoro: A Kansas Magazine
Topeka   KS
1891 - 1896

Alabama Sportsman
Birmingham   AL
1924 - 1927

Alaska Magazine
Juneau   AK
1927 - Unkwn

Alaska Monthly Magazine
Juneau   AK
1906 - 1907
Earlier Title: Alaska Monthly; An
Illustrated Magazine

Alaska Sportsman
Ketchikan   AK
1935 - Unkwn

Alaska-Yukon Magazine
Juneau   AK
1905 - 1912
Earlier Title: Alaska's Magazine

Alaskan Magazine
Juneau   AK
1947 - Unkwn

*Alaskan Magazine; the Occident
and Orient*
Tacoma   WA
1900 - Unkwn
Earlier Title: Alaskan Magazine
and Canadian Yukoner

*Albany Bouquet; and Literary
Spectator*
Albany   NY
1835

*Alleghany Magazine, or Repository
of Useful Knowledge*
Meadville   PA
1816 - 1817

Arizona Magazine
Yuma   AZ
1893

Arizona Magazine
Tucson   AZ
1937

Arizona Wild Life Magazine
Bisbee   AZ
1928 - 1938
Earlier Title: Arizona Wildlife and
Sportsman

Arizona Woman
Phoenix   AZ
1930 - 1934

*Arizona; The State Magazine and
Pathfinder*
Phoenix   AZ
1910 - 1925

Arkansas
Fayetteville   AR
1913 - 1920

Arkansas Magazine
Little Rock   AR
1854

Arkansas Sketch Book
Little Rock   AR
1896 - 1913

Arkansas Sketch Book
Little Rock   AR
1906 - 1910
Earlier Title: Little Rock Sketch
Book and as Sketch Book

Arkansas Thomas Cat, The
Hot Springs   AR
1890 - 1948

Arkansas Traveler
Little Rock   AR
1882 - 1916

Atlantic Sportsman
Winston-Salem NC
1931 - 1933

Aurora. A Southern Literary Magazine
Memphis   TN
1858 - 1861

Baltimore Literary Monument
Baltimore   MD
1838 - 1839
Earlier Title: Baltimore Monument

Baltimore Magazine
Baltimore   MD
1807

Baltimore Magazine and Literary Repository
Baltimore   MD
1804 - 1805
Earlier Title: Orphan's Friend and Literary Repository

Baltimore Monument
Baltimore   MD
1836 - 1838
Earlier Title: Baltimore Literary Monument

Baltimore Weekly Magazine
Baltimore   MD
1800 - 1801

Baltimore Weekly Magazine, and Ladies Miscellany
Baltimore   MD
1818

Bay State Magazine; Exponent of Universal Cheer and Efficiency
Boston   MA
1914 - 1915

Bay View Magazine; An Illustrated Monthly
Detriot   MI
1893 - 1922
Earlier Title: Bay View Reflector

Beautiful Florida
Winter Park   FL
1924 - 1931

Boston Kaleidoscope and Literary Rambler
Boston   MA
1818 - 1819

Boston Literary Magazine
Boston   MA
1832 - 1833

Boston Magazine
Boston   MA
1783 - 1786

Boston Magazine
Boston   MA
1802 - 1806
Earlier Title: Boston Weekly Magazine

Boston Monthly Magazine
Boston   MA
1825 - 1826

Boston Spectator and Ladies Album
Boston   MA
1826 - 1827
Earlier Title: Boston Spectator

Boston Spectator; Devoted to
Politicks and Belles-Lettres
Boston   MA
1814 - 1815
Earlier Title: Boston Spectator
and Ladies Album

Boston Transcript
Boston   MA
1946

Boston Weekly Magazine
Boston   MA
1743

Boston Weekly Magazine
Boston   MA
1816 - 1824

Boston Weekly Magazine
Boston   MA
1838 - 1841

Bostonian
Boston   MA
1894 - 1896

Bostonian; A Monthly Magazine
Boston   MA
1909 - 1910
Earlier Title: Bostonia

Bostonian, The
Boston   MA
1927 - 1930

Brooklyn Life
Brooklyn   NY
1890 - 1931

Brooklyn Monthly
Brooklyn   NY
1877 - 1879

Brooklyn New Monthly Magazine
Brooklyn   NY
1880

Bystander, The
Cleveland   OH
1921 - 1934
Earlier Title: Town and Country
Club News

California Cactus; A Monthly
Magazine Published in Interests
of the Negro Race
Los Angeles   CA
1910 - 1911

California Illustrated Magazine
San Francisco CA
1891 - 1894

California Magazine
Los Angeles   CA
1904 - 1906
Earlier Title: Traveler's Blue Book

California Magazine and
Mountaineer
San Francisco CA
1861 - 1863
Earlier Title: California
Mountaineer

California Mountaineer
San Francisco CA
1861

California Out-of-doors
San Francisco CA
1914 - Unkwn
Earlier Title: Tamalpais Magazine

California Outdoors
Los Angeles   CA
1921 - Unkwn

California Traveler
San Francisco CA
1932 - Unkwn

California Traveller and Naturalist
San Jose   CA
1892 - 1893
Earlier Title: Traveller and
Naturalist

Californian and Overland Monthly
San Francisco CA
1880 - 1882

Cambridge Magazine
Cambridge   MA
1896

Camden Miscellany
Camden   SC
1847 - Unkwn

Cape Cod Magazine
Wareham   MA
1915 - 1928

Carolinas
Asheville   NC
1905

Carolinian; a Free Lance Magazine
Wilmington   NC
1912 - 1913

Charleston Observer, The
Charleston   SC
1827 - 1845

*Charleston Spectator, and Ladies
Literary Port Folio*
Charleston   SC
1806

*Chicago Magazine of Fashion, Mu-
sic and Home Reading*
Chicago   IL
1870 - 1876

*Chicago Magazine. The West As
It Is*
Chicago   IL
1857

*Chicago To-day; The Metropolitan
News Magazine*
Chicago   IL
1927 - 1930

Chicagoan
Chicago   IL
1868 - 1869

Chicagoan
Chicago   IL
1926 - 1935

*Chicora, or Messenger of the
South*
Charleston   SC
1842

*Cincinnati Mirror and Ladies'
Parterre*
Cincinnati   OH
1832 - 1833

*Cincinnati Mirror, and Western
Gazette of Literature, Science,
and the Arts*
Cincinnati   OH
1831 - 1836

*Cincinnati Miscellany; or, Antiq-
uities of the West*
Cincinnati   OH
1844 - 1846

Clevelander
Cleveland   OH
1926 - Unkwn

Colorado Magazine
Denver   CO
1893

Colorado Monthly
Denver   CO
1871 - 1872

Colorado Woman
Denver   CO
1894 - 1895
Earlier Title: Tourney Magazine

Columbus Today
Columbus   OH
1925 - 1938

Coming Country; An Illustrated
Monthly Magazine
St. Louis   MO
1904 - 1913

Connecticut Circle; The Magazine
of the Nutmeg State
New London   CT
1938 - Unkwn

Connecticut Lore
Portland   CT
1933 - 1934

Connecticut Magazine
Hartford   CT
1895-1908

    Earlier Title: Connecticut
    Quarterly

Connecticut Magazine
New Britain   CT
1922 - 1927

Connecticut Magazine; or, Gentle-
man's and Lady's Monthly Museum
Bridgeport   CT
1801

Courant. A Southern Literary
Journal
Columbia   SC
1859

Crossroads of the Pacific
Honolulu   HI
1910 - 1912

Cumberland Empire; A Magazine
of Lore and Legend
Big Laurel   VA
1932 - 1933

Cumberland Magazine; or,
Whitehaven Monthly
Whitehaven   IA
1779 - 1781

Cumberland Monthly. A Magazine
of Popular Miscellany
Brunswick   ME
1884 - 1886

Dacotah Magazine
Aberdeen   SD
1907 - 1909

Dallasite
Dallas   TX
1929 - 1930

Delaware Life
Wilmington   DE
1902

Delaware Magazine
Wilmington   DE
1908 - 1912
Earlier Title: New Amstel Magazine

Delaware State Magazine
Wilmington   DE
1919 - 1920
Earlier Title: Delaware Magazine

Delta Weekly; A Journal of Fact
and Opinion
Greenville   MS
1937 - 1938

Detroit Magazine
Detroit   MI
1946

Dixie
Jacksonville   FL
1910 - 1917

Dixie Sportsman
Knoxville   TN
1946 - Unkwn

Dixie; A Monthly Magazine
Baltimore   MD
1899 - 1900

Dixie; The Magazine of Southern Progress
Charleston   SC
1947 - 1948
Earlier Title: Dixie Handbook

Dixieana; The All-Southern Magazine
Louisville   KY
1937

Dixieland; the Illustrated Home Magazine of the South
Dallas   TX
1904 - Unkwn

Down in Dixie
New Orleans   LA
1896

East Side
New York   NY
1909 - 1914

East Texas Magazine
Longview   TX
1926 - Unkwn

Eastern Magazine
Bangor   ME
1835 - 1836
Earlier Title: Maine Monthly Magazine

Eastern Shore Magazine
Easton   MD
1937 - 1938

Echo; A Magazine Devoted to Society, Literature and Stage in the South
Richmond   VA
1902

Everglade Magazine
Miami   FL
1910 - 1915

Fetter's Southern Magazine
Louisville   KY
1892 - 1895
Earlier Title: Southern Magazine and Mid-Continent Magazine

Flatbush Magazine
Brooklyn   NY
1915 - Unkwn

Florida Life
Jacksonsville FL
1893 - Unkwn

Florida Magazine
Jacksonville   FL
1900 - 1903
Earlier Title: Sunny Lands

Florida Outdoors
Sanford   FL
1924 - 1926

Fort Worth
Fort Worth   TX
1928 - Unkwn

Frontier; A Magazine of the West
Denver   CO
1902 - 1906
Earlier Title: Garden of the Gods
Magazine

Georgia
Atlanta   GA
1925 - 1930

Golden Era
San Diego   GA
1852 - 1893

*Golden Gate; A Monthly Magazine
of the West*
Oakland   CA
1902

Golden West Magazine
Waterloo   IA
1909

Granite State Monthly
Manchester   NH
1877 - 1930
Earlier Title: New Hampshire; The
Granite State Monthly

Great Divide
Denver   CO
1889 - 1896

*Great Southwest; A Magazine of
Romance, History and Progress*
Denver   CO
1906 - 1911

Great West
Kansas City   MO
1888 - 1889
Earlier Title: Kansas Magazine

Greater Chicago Magazine
Chicago   IL
1920 - 1923

Greater Chicago Magazine
Chicago   IL
1926 - Unkwn

Greater Cleveland
Cleveland   OH
1923 - Unkwn

Greater Pittsburgh
Pittsburgh   PA
1919 - 1926
Earlier Title: Pittsburgh First

Greater Portland
Portland   OR
1913

Greater St. Louis
St. Louis   MO
1919 - Unkwn

Greater Washington
Washington   DC
1933

Green Mountain Emporium
Montpelier   VT
1840 - 1842

Green Mountain Gem
Bradford   VT
1843 - 1849

Gulf Coast Magazine
Kingsville   TX
1905 - 1912
Earlier Title: Gulf Coast Line
Magazine

Gulf Coast Sportsman
Houston   TX
1930 - 1931

Harbinger of the Mississippi Valley
Frankfort   KY
1832

*Hawaii, A Magazine of News and
Comment*
Honolulu   HI
1940 - 1946

Hawaiian
Honolulu   HI
1872

Hawaiian
Honolulu   HI
1895 - 1896

*Holland's, The Magazine of the
South*
Dallas   TX
1876 - Unkwn
Earlier Title: Holland's Magazine
and as Street's Weekly

Hollywood Magazine, The
Hollywood   FL
1925 - Unkwn

Hoosier Magazine
Indianapolis   IN
1929 - 1931

Hoosier Outdoors
Indianapolis   IN
1919 - 1920

*Hoosier; A Monthly Magazine for
Those Who Love the Truth*
Indianapolis   IN
1906 - Unkwn

Houston Gargoyle
Houston   TX
1928 - 1932
Earlier Title: Houston's New
Weekly

Hudson River Magazine
Hudson   NY
1938 - 1941
Earlier Title: Magazine of the
Hudson Valley

*Hutchinson's Illustrated California
Magazine*
San Francisco CA
1856 - 1861

Illinois Monthly Magazine
Cincinnati   OH
1830 - 1832
Earlier Title: Western Monthly
Magazine

*Illinois Statesman.   A Weekly
Magazine for Illinois*
Springfield   IL
1911

Illinois Wildlife
Champaign   IL
1945 - Unkwn

Illustrated Kentuckian
Lexington   KY
1892 - 1900

Illustrated South Florida
Orlando   FL
1894 - Unkwn

Illustrated Southern Kansas
Lawrence   KS
1886

Illustrated West
Grand Encampme WY
1902

Illustrated West Shore
Spokane   WA
1875 - 1891
Earlier Title: West Shore

*Indiana Past and Present; A Mag-
azine of Hoosier Progress*
Indianapolis   IN
1914

Indiana Weekly
Indianapolis   IN
1895 - 1902
Earlier Title: Indiana Woman

Indianian; An Illustrated Monthly Magazine
Indianapolis   IN
1897 - 1901

Inland Monthly Magazine
St. Louis   MO
1872 - 1878

Iowa Magazine
Des Moines   IA
1916 - 1922

Islander
Honolulu   HI
1875

Islander
Honolulu   HI
1937 - 1949
Earlier Title: New Islander

Jamestown Magazine
Norfolk   VA
1906 - 1907

Kansas Citian
Kansas City   MO
1912 - Unkwn

Kansas Magazine
Topeka   KS
1872 - 1873

Kansas Magazine
Wichita   KS
1909 - 1912

Kansas Monthly
Lawrence   KS
1878 - 1883

Kentucky Magazine
Lexington   KY
1916 - 1918

Lee's Texas Magazine
Dallas   TX
1893 - 1906
Earlier Title: The Period

Lexington Literary Journal
Lexington   KY
1833

Literary Magnolia, A Southern Family Journal
Richmond   VA
1852

Long Island Home Journal, the Village Life Magazine
Long Island   NY
1914

Long Island Magazine
Long Island   NY
1903 - Unkwn

Louisiana. Journal Politique, Litteraire at Compagnard
Gentilly   LA
1865 - Unkwn

Louisville Monthly Magazine
Louisville   KY
1879 - 1880

M'lle New York
New York   NY
1895 - 1899

Magazine of Michigan
East Lansing   MI
1929 - 1931

*Magnolia; or, Southern
Appalachian*
Charleston   SC
1840 - 1843

*Magnolia: A Southern Home
Journal*
Richmond   VA
1862 - 1864

Maine Magazine
Lewistown   ME
1906 - 1907

Maine Monthly Magazine
Portland   ME
1836 - 1837
Earlier Title: Portland Magazine

Maine Sportsman
Bangor   ME
1893 - 1908

Maine State Magazine
Portland   ME
1873 - 1874

Manhattan Monthly
New York   NY
1869 - 1877

*Manhattan.   An Illustrated Liter-
ary Magazine*
New York   NY
1883 - 1884

*Manhattan; A Weekly for Wakeful
New Yorkers*
New York   NY
1933

Maryland Magazine
Baltimore   MD
1794

*Maryland Monthly Magazine; An
Illustrated Monthly*
Reisterstown   MD
1906 - 1907

*Massachusetts Magazine, or
Monthly Museum*
Boston   MA
1789 - 1796

*Massachusetts Magazine, Devoted
to the Literature and History of
the Bay State*
Boston   MA
1884 - 1887

*Mercury, Devoted to Polite
Southern Literature*
Raleigh   NC
1860 - Unkwn

*Metropolis; A Magazine of the City
of New York*
New York   NY
1921

*Metropolis; A Weekly Magazine for
New York Hotel Guests*
New York   NY
1920 - 1941

Michigan Sportsman
Detroit   MI
1914 - 1923
Earlier Title: Shiawassee County
Sportsman

Michigan Sportsman
Lansing   MI
1933

Michigan Women
Detroit   MI
1923 - 1931

Mid-Continent
Denver   CO
1909 - 1912
Earlier Title: Greater Colorado Illustrated

Mid-Continent Magazine
Louisville   KY
1892 - 1895
Earlier Title: Fetter's Southern
Magazine

*Mid-West Story. A Regional
Journal of the Old Northwest*
Vincennes   IN
1931 - 1937
Earlier Title: Mid-West Story
Magazine

Midland and Milwaukee Magazine
Milwaukee   WI
1871 - 1877
Earlier Title: Whittaker's Illustrated Milwaukee Magazine

Midland Monthly Magazine
Des Moines   IA
1894 - 1899

*Midland. A Magazine of the Mid-
dle West*
Chicago   IL
1915 - 1933

Milwaukee Literary Messenger
Milwaukee   WI
1869 - 1874

Minnesota Monthly
St. Paul   MN
1869 - 1870

Minnesota Sportsman's Digest
Minneapolis   MN
1940 - 1948
Earlier Title: Minnesota
Conservationist and Sportsman's
Digest

*Miscellaneous Portfolio; or South-
ern Weekly Magazine of Belles -
Lettres*
Maryville   TN
1839 - Unkwn

Miscellany, The
New Orleans   LA
1887 - 1889

Mississippi Palladium
Holly Springs MS
1851 - 1852

Mississippi Valley Magazine
St. Louis   MO
1919 - 1932

Mississippi Valley Sportsman
Memphis   TN
1947 - Unkwn

Missouri Magazine
Kansas City   MO
1915

Missouri Magazine
Jefferson City MO
1928 - 1938
Earlier Title: Missouriana

Missouriana
Jefferson City MO
1938 - 1940

Montana Wildlife
Helena   MT
1928 - 1932

Nantucket Weekly Magazine
Nantucket   MA
1817 - 1818

Native Virginian
Orange   VA
1867 - 1869

Nebraska Homes
Bloomington   NE
1885 - 1886

Nebraska's Own Magazine
Omaha   NE
1929 - 1931

Nevada Magazine
Winnemucca   NV
1899 - 1900

Nevada Magazine
Minden   NV
1945 - Unkwn

New England Magazine
Boston   MA
1831 - 1835

*New England Magazine of Know-
ledge and Pleasure*
Boston   MA
1758 - 1759

*New England Magazine; An Illus-
trated Monthly*
Boston   MA
1884 - 1917
Earlier Title: Bay State Monthly

New England Pictorial
Boston   MA
1881

New England Sportsman
Cambridge   MA
1931 - 1933

New Hampshire Magazine
Concord   NH
1793

New Hampshire Magazine
Manchester   NH
1843 - 1844

New Hampshire Sportsman
Manchester   NH
1947 - 1948

*New Haven Gazette and the
Connecticut Magazine*
New Haven   CT
1786 - 1789

New Jersey Life
Plainfield   NJ
1931

New Jersey Magazine
New Brunswick NJ
1786 - 1787

New Jersey Magazine
Newark   NJ
1841

New Jersey Magazine
Newark   NJ
1907

New Orleanian
New Orleans   LA
1930 - Unkwn

New Orleans Life
New Orleans   LA
1925 - 1927

New Orleans Magazine, The
New Orleans   LA
1898

New Orleans Miscellany
New Orleans   LA
1847 - 1848

New Orleans Noesis
New Orleans   LA
1854 - Unkwn

New South
Port Royal   SC
1862 - 1864

New South
Dallas   TX
1912 - 1913

New South; A Journal of Pro-
gressive Opinion
Birmingham   AL
1936 - Unkwn

New South, A Magazine of Southern Thought and Opportunity
Chattanooga   TN
1927

New St. Louis Magazine
St. Louis   MO
1871 - 1896
Earlier Title: St. Louis Ladies'
Magazine, St. Louis Magazine

New York Ledger
New York   NY
1844 - 1903
Earlier Title: Household-Ledger

New York Literary Journal, and
Belles-Lettres Repository
New York   NY
1819 - 1821
    Earlier Title: Belles-Lettres
    Repository, and Monthly Mag-
    azine

New York Magazine
New York   NY
1929 - 1930

New York Magazine; A Rochester
New Monthly
Rochester   NY
1853

New York Magazine, and General
Repository of Useful Knowledge
New York   NY
1814

New York Magazine, or Literary
Repository
New York   NY
1790 - 1797

New York Monthly
New York   NY
1854

New York Monthly Magazine
New York   NY
1824

New York Quarterly Magazine
New York   NY
1836 - 1837

New York Sportsman
New York   NY
1875 - 1892

New York Woman
New York   NY
1936 - 1937

New Yorker
Westfield   NJ
1910 - 1912

New Yorker
New York   NY
1901 - 1906

New Yorker; A Complete Mirror
of the World
New York   NY
1858 - 1859

Nor' Wester; A Magazine for the
Pacific Northwest
Seattle   WA
1939

*North Carolina Magazine, or Uni-
versal Intelligencer*
Newbern   NC
1764 - 1765

*North Carolina Magazine: Poli-
tical, Historical, and Miscellaneous*
Unknwn   NC
1813

North Dakota Outdoors
Bismark   ND
1938 - Unkwn

North Star
Sitka   AL
1887 - 1898
Earlier Title: Northern Light

Northern Monthly
Newark   NJ
1867 - 1868
Earlier Title: New Jersey Magazine

Northland Magazine
Minneapolis   MN
1898 - Unkwn

Northwest Life
Minneapolis   MN
1927 - Unkwn

Northwest Magazine
St. Paul   MN
1897 - 1932
Earlier Title: Western Magazine

*Northwest Magazine; An
Exploitative Monthly Devoted to
the Pacific Northwest*
Boise   ID
1906

Ohio Magazine
Columbus   OH
1906 - 1908

Ohio Magazine
Columbus   OH
1944 - 1948

Ohio Sportsman
Cincinnati   OH
1923 - 1925

Ohio Woman
Columbus   OH
1911 - 1917

Oklahoma Magazine
Oklahoma City OH
1905 - 1912

*Oklahoma Magazine; A Journal of
Oklahoma and the Indian Territory*
Oklahoma City OK
1893 - 1895

Oklahoma Wildlife
Oklahoma City OK
1945 - Unkwn
Earlier Title: Oklahoma Game and
Fish News

*Old Dominion. A Monthly Maga-
zine of Literature, Science and
Art*
Richmond   VA
1867 - 1873

Omaha's Own Magazine
Omaha   NB
1926 - 1931

Oregon Magazine
Salem   OR
1918 - Unkwn

Oregon Monthly Magazine
Portland   OR
1851

Oregon Sportsman
Portland   OR
1913 - 1927

*Orion, or Southern Monthly: A
Magazine of Original Literature*
Penfield   GA
1842 - 1844

Orleanian, The
New Orleans   LA
1927 - 1928

Out West
Los Angeles   CA
1894 - 1923

Out West
Colorado Sprin CO
1873

Out West Magazine
Helena   MT
1949 - Unkwn
Earlier Title: Montana Treasure
Magazine

Outdoor California
Sacramento   CA
1930 - Unkwn

Outdoor Nebraskaland
Lincoln   NB
1926 - Unkwn
Earlier Title: Outdoor Nebraska

Outdoor West
Sacramento   CA
1919 - Unkwn

*Outdoor West; The Sierra
Sportsman*
Reno   NV
1932 - Unkwn

*Overland Monthly and Out West
Magazine*
San Francisco CA
1868 - 1935

Ozark Life Outdoors
Kingston   AR
1925 - 1932
Earlier Title: Ozark Life

Ozark Magazine
Romance   AR
1935

Pacific Coast Golfer
Seattle   WA
1926 - Unkwn
Earlier Title: Northwest Golfer

Pacific Magazine
Seattle   WA
1889 - 1891
Earlier Title: Washington Magazine

Pacific Monthly
Los Angeles   CA
1889 - 1891

Pacific Monthly
Whittier   CA
1928 - 1938

Pacific Monthly
Portland   OR
1898 - 1911
Earlier Title: Sunset

*Pacific Monthly; Devoted to the
Arts, Science, Literature and Life*
San Francisco CA
1858 - 1864
Earlier Title: Hesperian

Pacific Northwesterner
Spokan   WA
1946 - Unkwn

Pacific Sportsman
San Francisco CA
1925 - Unkwn

*Pacific Sportsman; The Outdoor
Magazine of the Pacific Northwest*
Seattle   WA
1904 - 1907
Earlier Title: Pacific Coast
Sportsman

Parade
Cleveland   OH
1931 - 1932
Earlier Title: Cleveland Mid-Week
Review Pictorial

Pennsylvania Magazine
Harrisburg   PA
1857

*Pennsylvania Magazine; or, Amer-
ican Monthly Museum*
Philadelphia   PA
1775 - 1776

Peoples Magazine of Arizona
Phoenix   AZ
1938 - 1939
Earlier Title: Arizona Homes and
Gardens

*Philadelphia Magazine and Weekly
Repository*
Philadelphia   PA
1818

*Philadelphia Magazine; A Hand-
some Repository of Literary Ex-
cellence*
Philadelphia   PA
1877 - 1885

*Philadelphia Magazine, or, Uni-
versal Repository of Knowledge*
Philadelphia   PA
1798

Philadelphia Monthly Magazine
Philadelphia   PA
1827 - 1830

Philadelphia Monthly Magazine
Philadelphia   PA
1854 - 1859

Philadelphia Museum and Review
Philadelphia   PA
1799

Pictorial California and the Pacific
Los Angeles   CA
1925 - Unkwn
Earlier Title: Pictorial California

Pittsburgh Bulletin Index
Pittsburgh   PA
1930 - 1949

*Plantation: A Southern Quarterly
Journal*
Eatonton   GA
1860

Portland Magazine
Portland   ME
1805

Portland Magazine
Portland   ME
1834 - 1836
Earlier Title: Maine Monthly Magazine

Rhode Island Literary Repository
Providence   RI
1814 - 1815

Richmond Eclectic
Richmond   VA
1866 - 1875

Richmond Literary Miscellany
Richmond   VA
1883

Rochester Gem, and Ladies'
Amulet
Rochester   NY
1829 - 1843
Earlier Title: Gem and Rochester
Mirror

Rochester Monthly Miscellany
Rochester   NY
1881

Rocky Mountain Life
Denver   CO
1946 - 1949

Rocky Mountain Magazine
Denver   CO
1903 - 1906

Rocky Mountain Magazine
Helena   MT
1900 - 1902

Rural Carolinian
Charleston   SC
1869 - 1876

Rural Southland
New Orleans   LA
1869 - 1873

Sacramento Valley Monthly
Sacramento   CA
1911 - 1924

Salt Lake Outlook. An Illustrated
Monthly Magazine
Salt Lake City UT
1908 - 1909

San Antonian; Voice of the Cham-
ber of Commerce
San Antonio   TX
1916 - Unkwn

San Franciscan, The
San Francisco CA
1927 - Unkwn

Santa Fean
Santa Fe   NM
1940 - 1942

Scene; Magazine of the South and
West
Dallas   TX
1947

Scenic Idaho
Boise   ID
1946 - Unkwn

Script
Los Angeles   CA
1929 - 1949
Earlier Title: Rob Wagner's Script

Senator
Washington   DC
1939

Sky-Land; Stories of Picturesque
North Carolina
Charlotte   NC
1913 - 1915

Smalley's Magazine
St. Paul   MN
1883 - 1903
Earlier Title: Northwest and
Northwest Illustrated Monthly
Magazine

South
Hollywood   FL
1924 - 1927

South
Richmond   VA
1857 - 1858

South Atlantic. A Monthly Magazine of Literature, Science, and Art
Wilmington   NC
1877 - 1882

South Carolina Museum
Charleston   SC
1797 - 1798

South Carolina State Magazine
Aiken   SC
1911

South Dakotan
Mitchell   SD
1898 - 1904
Earlier Title: Monthly South Dakotan

South Illustrated, The
New Orleans   LA
1886 - 1889

South; The Magazine of Travel
New Orleans   LA
1945 - 1948

South-Western American
Austin   TX
1852

Southampton Magazine
Southampton   NY
1912 - 1913

Southern and Western Monthly Magazine and Review
Charleston   SC
1845

Southern Confederacy
Atlanta   GA
1863 - Unkwn

Southern Dial
Montgomery   AL
1857 - 1858

Southern Eclectic
Augusta   GA
1853 - 1854

Southern Eclectic Magazine
Charleston   SC
1850

Southern Field and Fireside
Augusta   GA
1859 - 1864

Southern Friend
Richmond   VA
1864 - 1866

Southern Garden
New Orleans   LA
1894 - 1895

Southern Garden
Raleigh   NC
1938 - 1941

Southern Golf Magazine
Atlanta   GA
1923 - 1927
Earlier Title: Outdoors-South

Southern Golfer
Jacksonville   FL
1920 - 1928
Earlier Title: Metropolitan Golfer

Southern Highlander
Rome   GA
1907 - Unkwn

Southern Homes
Columbia   SC
1904 - 1905

Southern Homestead
Nashville   TN
1858

Southern Ladies Book; a Magazine
of Literature, Science and Arts
Charleston   SC
1840 - 1843
Earlier Title: Magnolia; or,
Southern Appalachian

Southern Lady's Book
New Orleans   LA
1852 - 1853

Southern Lady's Companion
Nashville   TN
1847 - 1854

Southern Lady's Magazine
Baltimore   MD
1850

Southern Life, Home and Garden
Magazine
Raleigh   NC
1938 - 1941
Earlier Title: Southern Garden

Southern Literary Companion
Newman   GA
1859 - 1864

Southern Literary Gazette
Charleston   SC
1848 - 1855

Southern Literary Journal
Oxford   GA
1850

Southern Literary Magazine, The
Nashville   TN
1923 - 1924
Earlier Title: The Southern Magazine

Southern Literary Messenger
Richmond   VA
1834 - 1864

Southern Literary Register
Columbia   SC
1820

Southern Magazine
Manassas   VA
1899

Southern Magazine
Richmond   VA
1906 - 1907

Southern Magazine and Monthly
Review
Petersburg   VA
1841

Southern Magazine, The
New Orleans   LA
1898

Southern Miscellany, A Monthly
Devoted to Literature in the South
Montgomery   AL
1915 - 1916

Southern Monthly
Memphis   TN
1861 - 1862

Southern Monthly Magazine
New Orleans   LA
1869

Southern Parlor Magazine
Memphis   TN
1851 - 1856

Southern Past and Literary
Aspirant
Macon   GA
1837 - 1842

Southern Plantation
Montgomery   AL
1874 - 1877

Southern Portfolio
Richmond   VA
1866 - Unkwn

Southern Punch
Richmond   VA
1863 - 1864

Southern Rose
Charleston   SC
1832 - 1839

Southern Scribe, A Magazine About People
New Orleans   LA
1909 - 1911

Southern Son
Nashville   TN
1868

Southern Sportsman
New Orleans   LA
1843

Southern Tribute.   A Monthly Magazine
Austin   TX
1897 - 1898

Southern Woman's Magazine
Nashville   TN
1913 - 1918

Southerner
Lynchburg   VA
1927 - 1931

Southland
Waco   TX
1892 - Unkwn

Southland Magazine.   A Magazine of the South
Norfolk   VA
1901 - 1910

Southland, The
Salisbury   NC
1890 - 1891

Southron
Tuscaloosa   AL
1839

Southron, or, Lily of the Valley
Gallatin   TX
1841

Southwest Magazine of Texas
Fort Worth   TX
1904 - Unkwn

Southwest Monthly
Pulaski   VA
1909

Southwest Texas Magazine
Beeville   TX
1894

Southwest Today
Phoenix   AZ
1906 - 1907
Earlier Title: Arizona Magazine

Southwestern Journal: A Magazine of Science, Literature and Miscellany
Natchez   MS
1837 - 1838

Southwestern Literary Journal and Monthly Review
Nashville   TN
1844 - 1845

*Southwestern Magazine, Devoted
to Literature, Art, and the Pros-
perity...*
New Orleans   LA
1866

Southwestern Monthly
Nashville   TN
1852

Spirit of the Old Dominion
Richmond   VA
1829

Spirit of the South
Eufaula   AL
1851

St. Louis Life
St. Louis   MO
1889 - 1897

St. Paul
St. Paul   MN
1929 - 1932
Earlier Title: St. Paul Magazine

Sun Colony
Ft. Lauderdale FL
1945 - Unkwn

Sun-up, Maine's Own Magazine
Portland   ME
1925 - 1932
Earlier Title: Maine's Own Magazine

Sunny South
Jacksonville   AL
1851

Sunny South
Atlanta   GA
1875 - 1903

Tennessee Monthly Museum
Franklin   TN
1831 - Unkwn

Texas Magazine
Austin   TX
1896 - 1898

Texas Magazine, The
Houston   TX
1909 - 1913

Texas Monthly
Dallas   TX
1928 - 1930
Earlier Title: Bunker's Monthly

Texas Siftings
Austin   TX
1882 - 1897

Texas Wild Life
Austin   TX
1936

Town Tidings
Buffalo   NY
1927 - 1937

Town Topics
New York   NY
1885 - 1937

Utah Fish and Game Magazine
Salt Lake City UT
1946 - Unkwn

*Utah Magazine; the Home Journal
of the People*
Salt Lake City UT
1868 - 1869

Utah Monthly Magazine
Salt Lake City UT
1884 - 1895

Vermont Monthly
West Randolph   VT
1888 - 1889

*Virginia Historical Register and
Literary Companion*
Richmond   VA
1848 - 1853

Virginia Magazine
Lynchburg   VA
1908 - 1909

Virginia Spectator
Charlottesvill VA
1838 - 1839

Virginias
Staunton   VA
1880 - 1885

Washington Literary Gazette
Washington   DC
1832 - 1837
Earlier Title: Metropolitan

Washington Mirror
Washington   DC
1899 - 1905

*Washington Quarterly Magazine of
Arts, Science and Literature*
Washington   DC
1823 - 1824

Washington Sportsman
Seattle   WA
1935 - 1938
Earlier Title: Rocky Mountain
Sportsman

*Washingtonian; A State Magazine
of Progress*
Seattle   WA
1928 - 1929

West Coast Sportsman
San Francisco   CA
1948 - Unkwn

West Coast; An Illustrated Monthly
Los Angeles   CA
1906 - 1914
Earlier Title: West Coast Magazine

Westchester Countryside
White Plains   NY
1936 - 1938

Westchester Life
New Rochelle   NY
1926 - 1938

Westchester Magazine
Pleasantville NY
1929 - 1932

Western Homes and Gardens
San Jose   CA
1915 - 1932
Earlier Title: Pacific Grower

*Western Literary and Historical
Magazine*
Louisville   KY
1842

Western Literary Magazine
Louisville   KY
1853 - Unkwn

Western Literary Magazine
Pittsburgh   PA
1840 - 1844

*Western Literary Magazine and
Journal of Education, Science,
Arts and Morals*
Detroit   MI
1849

Western Literary Magazine; A Literary Monthly
Chicago   IL
1845 - 1846

Western Luminary
Lexington   KY
1824 - 1835

Western Magazine
San Diego   CA
1906

Western Magazine and Louisville Literary Gazette
Louisville   KY
1838 - Unkwn
Earlier Title: Aegis

Western Monthly Magazine and Literary Journal
Cincinnati   OH
1833 - 1837
Earlier Title: Illinois Monthly Magazine

Western New England Magazine
Springfield   MA
1910 - 1913

Western Skier
Seattle   WA
1936 - 1939

Western Skiiing
Los Angeles   CA
1945 - 1948

Western Wild Life
Denver   CO
1933 - 1936

Western Woman
San Francisco CA
1906 - 1908
Earlier Title: Yellow Ribbon

Western Woman
Seattle   WA
1923 - 1928

Western World
San Francisco CA
1906 - 1907
Earlier Title: New San Francisco Magazine

Wheler's Southern Monthly Magazine
Athens   GA
1849 - 1850

Whitaker's Southern Magazine
Charleston   SC
1850 - 1853

White Mountain Echo and Tourists' Register
Bethlehem   NH
1878 - 1926

White Mountain Life
Littleton   NH
1897 - 1899

Whittaker's Milwaukee Magazine
Milwaukee   WI
1871 - 1877

Wisconsin Magazine
Madison   WI
1923 - 1932

Wisconsin Woman
Ashland   WI
1900 - 1901

Worcester Magazine
Worcester   MA
1786 - 1788

Wyoming Literary Monthly
Buffalo   WY
1881

Wyoming Wild Life
Cheyenne   WY
1936- 1938

Appendix B

List of Library Holdings Symbols (Arranged alphabetically by state)

Alabama

AAA	Auburn University
AMP	Mobile Public Library
ALM	University of Alabama
ABC	University of Alabama, Birmingham
MWR	University of Alabama, Huntsville

Arizona

AZS	Arizona State University
AZH	Flagstaff City Library
MSA	Mesa Public Library
AZN	Northern Arizona University
PNX	Phoenix Public Library
AZD	Scottsdale Public Library
ATM	Tempe Public Library
AZT	Tucson Public Library
AZU	University of Arizona

Arkansas

AST	Arkansas State Library
AKH	Henderson State University
AFU	University of Arkansas, Fayetteville
AKU	University of Arkansas, Little Rock
AKC	University of Central Arkansas

California

CIT	California Institute of Technology
CBA	California State College
CPO	California State Polytechnic University
CCH	California State University, Chico
CFI	California State University, Fullerton
CLO	California State University, Long Beach
CLA	California State University, Los Angeles
CNO	California State University, Northridge
CSA	California State University, Sacramento
HDC	Claremont College
CGE	El Segundo Public Library
CGN	Glendale College
CHU	Humboldt State University
CLB	Long Beach Public Library
JQW	Los Angeles County Public Library
LPU	Los Angeles Public Library
CNB	Newport Beach Public Library
CPP	Pasadena Public Library
CDS	San Diego State University
CSF	San Francisco State University
CSJ	San Jose State University
SMP	Santa Monica Public Library
GAS	Southern College of Technology
CUI	University of California, Irvine
CLU	University of California, Los Angeles
CUS	University of California, San Diego
CUT	University of California, Santa Barbara

CUZ   University of California, Santa Cruz
CUR   University of Redlands
CSL   University of Southern California

Colorado

DNH   Colorado Historical Society Library
COP   Colorado School of Mines
COF   Colorado State University
DPL   Denver Public Library
CDF   Ft. Lewis College
COG   Three Rivers Library System
COA   University of Colorado, Denver
DVP   University of Denver
COS   University of Southern Colorado

Connecticut

GMY   Bill Memorial Library, Groton
BPT   Bridgeport Public Library
CTL   Connecticut College
CZL   Connecticut State Library
CTW   Eastern Connecticut State University
FRP   Fairfield Public Library
HPL   Hartford Public Library
GPI   New Britain Public Library
NHP   New Haven Free Public Library
UBM   University of Bridgeport
UCW   University of Connecticut
UCH   University of Connecticut, Health Center
GME   Village Library, Farmington
WHP   West Hartford Public Library
GWH   West Haven Public Library
CTD   Western Connecticut State University
YUS   Yale University

District of Columbia

FTC   Federal Trade Commission
DGW   George Washington University
DGU   Georgetown University
DHU   Howard University
DLC   Library of Congress
AGL   National Agriculture Library
SMI   Smithsonian Institution
DDU   University of the District of Columbia

Delaware

DLM   University of Delaware
DLB   Widener College, Delaware Campus

Florida

EDB   Broward Community College
FBR   Broward County Library
FGM   Florida Atlantic University

FJD	Florida Community College, Jacksonsville
FXG	Florida International University
FDA	Florida State University
DZM	Miami-Dade Public Library
ORL	Orange County Library System
FBA	State Library of Florida
FTU	University of Central Florida
FUG	University of Florida
FQG	University of Miami
FHM	University of South Florida

Georgia

GAP	Atlanta-Fulton Public Library
GJG	Augusta College
EMU	Emory University
GAT	Georgia Institute of Technology
GPM	Georgia Southern College
GSU	Georgia State University
GXM	Medical College of Georgia
GUA	University of Georgia

Hawaii

HUH	University of Hawaii
HIL	University of Hawaii, Hilo

Illinois

IBA	Bradley University
CRL	Center for Research Library, Chicago
IBF	Chicago Municipal Reference Library
CGP	Chicago Public Library
IAA	Chicago State Library
IBZ	Columbia College
IAC	DePaul University
IAF	Governors State University
IHV	Highland Park Public Library
ICG	Illinois Benedictine College
JFK	Illinois State Historical Library
SPI	Illinois State Library
ILM	Lincoln Library, Springfield
IAL	Loyola University of Chicago
IBV	Newberry Library
IAO	Northeastern Illinois University
JNA	Northern Illinois University
SOI	Southern Illinois University
UIL	University of Illinois

Indiana

IBS	Ball State University
IIB	Butler University
XCA	Carmel Public Library
ISL	Indiana State Library
XSU	Indiana State University
IUL	Indiana University

IUP   Indiana University--Purdue University, Indianapolis
IPL   Purdue University
IUE   University of Evansville
IND   University of Notre Dame

Iowa

JID   Des Moines Area Community College
IOQ   Iowa State Historical Society
IWA   Iowa State University
IOU   Public Library of Des Moines
IOV   University of Dubuque

Kansas

KKN   Kansas Newman College
KFP   Pittsburg State University
KSW   Wichita State University

Kentucky

KBE   Berea College
KCC   Centre College of Kentucky
KEU   Eastern Kentucky University
KUK   University of Kentucky

Louisiana

LDA   Amistad Research Center, Tulane University
CEN   Centenary College
LSM   Louisiana State University
LUU   Louisiana State University
LRT   Louisiana Tech University
LLM   Loyola University
LNC   New Orleans Public Library
LRU   Tulane University
LNU   University of New Orleans
LWA   University of Southwestern Louisiana

Maine

BYN   Bangor Public Library
BBH   Bowdoin College
MEA   Maine State Library
PPN   Portland Public Library
UMF   University of Maine, Farmington

Maryland

MFS   Frostburg State University
JHE   Johns Hopkins University
MDS   St. Mary's College of Maryland
BAL   University of Baltimore
UMC   University of Maryland

Massachusetts

FRQ	Acton Memorial Library
AQM	American Antiquarian Society
BET	Bentley College
BOS	Boston University
MBU	Boston University School of Medicine
BDR	Bridgewater State College
CXM	Centerville Public Library
CPY	Concord Public Library
DHP	Dedham Public Library
HLS	Harvard University
HUL	Harvard University
MAS	Massachusetts State Library
SCL	Simmons College
SMU	Southeastern Massachusetts University
SUF	Suffolk University
AUM	University of Massachusetts, Amherst
WPF	Wellesley Free Library
CXD	West Falmouth Library
WZW	Worcester Public Library

Michigan

EXC	Calvin College & Seminary
EHL	Clarke Historical Library, Mt. Pleasant
EYP	Detroit Public Library
EXR	Grand Rapids Public Library
EXG	Grand Valley State College
EEX	Library of Michigan, Lansing
EEM	Michigan State University
EZT	Michigan Technical University
EYD	University of Michigan, Dearborn
UMI	University Microfilm International, Ann Arbor
EYA	Washtenaw Community College
EYW	Wayne State University
EXW	Western Michigan University

Minnesota

DUD	Duluth Public Library
MHS	Minnesota Historical Society
MPI	Minneapolis Public Library
MNJ	St. John's University
MNO	St. Olaf College
SPP	St. Paul Public Library
MND	University of Minnesota, Duluth
MNU	University of Minnesota, Minneapolis
MNP	University of Minnesota, St. Paul
VAP	Virginia Public Library

Mississippi

MCD	Delta State University
MFM	Mississippi State University
MUM	University of Mississippi

Missouri

KCP	Kansas City Public Library
MNW	Northwest Missouri State University
SVP	St. Louis Public Library
MUU	University of Missouri

Nebraska

BCN	Bellevue College
LDL	University of Nebraska, Lincoln

New Hampshire

DRB	Dartmouth College
NHS	New Hampshire State Library
NHM	University of New Hampshire

New Jersey

ABR	Asbury Park Public Library
ACN	Atlantic City Library
NCL	Camden County Library
CMP	Cape May County Library
NJL	New Jersey State Library
PPR	Princeton Public Library
RID	Rider College
NJR	Rutgers University
TFP	Trenton Free Public Library

New Mexico

IPU	Eastern New Mexico University
NMS	New Mexico State Library
IRU	New Mexico State University
IQU	University of New Mexico

New York

XFN	Albany Public Library
YAM	American Museum of Natural History
VDB	Brooklyn College
VHB	Buffalo & Erie County Public Library
VKC	Canisius College
ZXC	City College (CUNY)
COO	Cornell University
VVH	Daemen College
SEU	East Hampton Free Library
VYF	Fordham University
YTR	George F. Johnson Memorial Library, Endicott
ZIH	Hofstra University
SFO	Huntington Public Library
VIO	Marlboro Library
NYB	Marymount College
VVX	Nassau Community College
NYP	New York Public Library
NYG	New York State Library

VVN   Niagra University
ZQP   Queens Borough Public Library
RVE   Rochester Institute of Technology
YQR   Rochester Public Library
SGQ   Rogers Memorial Library, Southampton
VVS   Sarah Lawrence College
VKM   Siena College
SYB   Syracuse University
NAM   SUNY at Albany
XFM   SUNY College, Fredonia
BUF   SUNY, Buffalo
RRR   University of Rochester
NYD   Westchester County Historical Society
VVW   Westchester Library System
SHI   Westhampton Free Library

North Carolina

NJB   Appalachian State University
NNM   Davidson College
NDD   Duke University
ERE   East Carolina University
NCS   North Carolina State Library
NRC   North Carolina State University
NPC   Public Library of Charlotte
NOC   University of North Carolina
NDO   University of North Carolina Law Library
NKM   University of North Carolina, Charlotte
NGU   University of North Carolina, Greensboro
EWF   Wake Forest University

North Dakota

UND   University of North Dakota

Ohio

ANC   Antioch College
BGU   Bowling Green State University
CHT   Cincinnati Historical Society Library
CLE   Cleveland Public Library
CSU   Cleveland State University
OGC   Grove City Public Library
KSU   Kent State University
OBE   Oberlin College
OHT   Ohio Historical Society
OUN   Ohio University
OCP   Public Library of Cincinnati
OCO   Public Library of Columbus
OHI   State Library of Ohio
CIN   University of Cincinnati
TOL   University of Toledo
UAP   Upper Arlington Public Library
YNG   Youngstown State University

Oklahoma

OKC   Cameron University
OKX   Central State University
OKN   Northeastern Oklahoma State University
OKS   Oklahoma State University
OKU   University of Oklahoma
OKT   University of Tulsa

Oregon

CEO   Central Oregon Community College
WAC   Dallas-Wasco County Public Library
DCH   Deschuter County Public Library
OEL   Eugene Public Library
JCL   Jackson County Library System
OHY   Oregon Historical Society Library
OSO   Oregon State Library, Salem
ORE   Oregon State University, Corvallis
OPU   Pacific University
OSE   Salem Public Library
OXY   Springfield Public Library
ORU   University of Oregon

Pennsylvania

PBU   Bucknell University
BUC   Bucks County Community College
DKC   Dickinson College
DXU   Drexel University
DUQ   Duquesne University
EAS   Eastern College
EPL   Erie County Library
PLF   Free Library of Philadelphia
LKC   Lancaster County Library
LAS   LaSalle University
LQS   Lock Haven University of Pennsylvania
UPM   Pennsylvania State University
SCR   Scranton Public Library
SRS   Slippery Rock University of Pennsylvania
PHA   State Library of Pennsylvania
PSC   Swarthmore College
TEU   Temple University
PAU   University of Pennsylvania
PIT   University of Pittsburgh
PVU   Villanova University

Rhode Island

RHI   Rhode Island Historical Society Library
RIU   University of Rhode Island

South Carolina

SGB   Bob Jones University
SXC   Charleston County Library
SEA   Clemson University

SBM   College of Charleston
SFU   Furman University
SGR   Greenville County Library
DSC   South Carolina State Library, Columbia
SUC   University of South Carolina
SWW   Winthrop College

South Dakota

SDS   South Dakota State Library, Pierre

Tennessee

TCN   Carson-Newman College
TKL   Knoxville Public Library
TMA   Memphis State University
TNN   Nashville Public Library
TNS   Tennessee State Library, Nashville
TKN   University of Tennessee
TJC   Vanderbilt University

Texas

TAP   Amarillo Public Library
TXG   Austin Public Library
IYU   Baylor University
CCA   Corpus Christi Public Library
IGA   Dallas Public Library
CDM   Del Mar College
IEA   East Texas State University
IFA   Fort Worth Public Library
TXN   Houston Public Library
TXR   Lamar University
INT   North Texas State University
TPN   Pan American University
SAP   San Antonio Public Library
ISM   Southern Methodist University
SNM   St. Mary's University
TXA   Texas A&M University
TXT   Texas Southern University
ILU   Texas Tech University
IWU   Texas Woman's University
TNY   Trinity University
TXH   University of Houston
IXA   University of Texas
IUA   University of Texas, Arlington
TXQ   University of Texas, Austin, Law Library
TXU   University of Texas, El Paso
TXJ   University of Texas, San Antonio
TWT   West Texas State University

Utah

UBY   Brigham Young University
UUM   University of Utah
ULC   Utah State Library
UUO   Weber State College

Vermont

VTU   University of Vermont
VTT   Vermont Law School

Virginia

VAX   Alexandria Public Library
VWM   College of William & Mary
AXL   Falls Church Public Library
VGM   George Mason University
VCQ   Lynchburg Public Library
VPW   Prince William Public Library
VRU   University of Richmond
VA@   University of Virginia
VPL   Virginia Beach Public Library
VRC   Virginia Commonwealth University
VMI   Virginia Military Institute
VPI   Virginia Polytechnic Institute & State University
VIC   Virginia State Library, Richmond
VLW   Washington & Lee University

Washington

WEA   Eastern Washington University
TAW   Tacoma Public Library
WAU   University of Washington

West Virginia

WVT   West Virginia Institute of Technology
WVU   West Virginia University

Wisconsin

WKG   Cardinal Stritch College
GZF   Eau Claire Public Library
WIM   Madison Public Library
WIW   Marathon County Public Library
WDA   Marinette County Library
GZQ   Marquette University
GZD   Milwaukee Public Library
WIH   State Historical Society of Wisconsin
GZU   University of Wisconsin, La Crosse
GZN   University of Wisconsin, Milwaukee

Wyoming

WYU   University of Wyoming

About the Compilers

SAMUEL G. RILEY is Professor in the Department of Communications Studies at Virginia Polytechnic Institute and State University. Dr. Riley is the author or editor of four other books: *Magazines of the American South, Index to Southern Magazines, American Magazine Journalists, 1741–1850,* and *American Magazine Journalists, 1850–1900.*

GARY W. SELNOW is Associate Professor in the Department of Communications Studies at Virginia Polytechnic Institute and State University. An active consultant and reviewer, Dr. Selnow is also the author of *Targeted Communication.*

www.ingramcontent.com/pod-product-compliance
Lightning Source LLC
Chambersburg PA
CBHW060349100426
42812CB00003B/1177

* 9 7 8 0 3 1 3 2 6 8 3 9 7 *